GROWING UP
WITH
JUST WILLIAM

by his sister

MARGARET DISHER

Margaret Disher

THE OUTLAWS PUBLISHING COMPANY
London, England

First published in Great Britain 1990

ISBN 0 9516261 0 8

Published in 1990 by
The Outlaws Publishing Company
The Old Barn, PO Box 3AD, London W1A 3AD

Associate companies in Arapkir, Arapongas, Cilnicu
Donja Stubica, Chayl, Janikowo, Kiparissia, Kopliku,
Mopipi, Mullumbimby, Onehunga and Quillabamba.

Typeset by I C Dawkins of London EC1
Printed and bound by Woolnough of Irthlingborough, Northants.

Contents

FAMILY TREE (1)

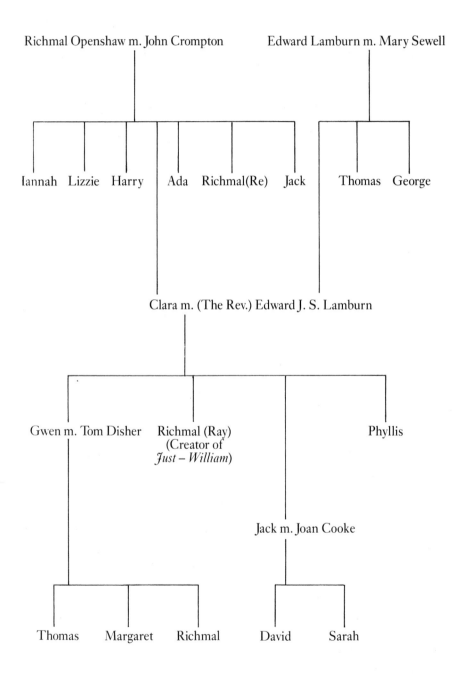

Richmal Openshaw m. John Crompton   Edward Lamburn m. Mary Sewell

Iannah   Lizzie   Harry   Ada   Richmal(Re)   Jack   Thomas   George

Clara m. (The Rev.) Edward J. S. Lamburn

Gwen m. Tom Disher   Richmal (Ray)   Phyllis
                       (Creator of
                       Just – William)

Jack m. Joan Cooke

Thomas   Margaret   Richmal   David   Sarah

Acknowledgements

I was pressurised into writing this book by a number of people – firstly by John Taylor, then journalist Audrey Whiting, with further encouragement from Ted Blackmore and Eric Merrill. Ruth Mirsky said: "Pretend you are telling me everything in a letter" – which is the way I have tried to recount the inside story of Just William and our family life.

I was delighted when Kay Williams, chronicler of our family history through her biography *Just-Richmal*, agreed to become the book's midwife, patiently editing as much as possible before I could change it back again! I am equally indebted to Roy Williams for his cover design, drawings and layout and for his invaluable help in restoring faded family snapshots, some of which were over 70 years old.

In addition to John Taylor there were other friends at the National Westminster Bank who provided further insights into Tommy's career, in particular Norman Shapton, Maurice Mason, Ivor Waters, Alan Goodrich, Frank O'Connor, J. O. Baxter, Hubert Peyton and G. A. Allen. The Rev. Douglas Redman added a (somewhat) more serious account of Tommy's adventures. My thanks go also to Jon Wynne-Tyson, whose advice and guidance on the mysteries of publishing made me realise I could do my own thing.

The Thomas Henry illustrations are reprinted with permission from Pan/Macmillan Children's Books, a division of Pan/Macmillan Ltd; copyright of the drawings is held by the Thomas Henry Estate. Photos of ponds at Keston and Bromley Common, also of Bromley Market Place, are reproduced with permission from the Bromley Central Library, Local Studies Department. John Filmer kindly allowed me to use his nostalgic map of Bromley Common and Len Smith added background information to aid my memory.

I should acknowledge how useful I found Lofts and Adley's *William – A Bibliography* in my attempts to locate individual stories within the books. Also my father's autobiography, *Sixty Odd Years*, gave me names of places I could not have remembered from my childhood; though I found some of his reminiscences more rose-coloured than my own (more accurate) memory of events.

M. D.   London

Richmal Crompton Lamburn in the 1920s

Richmal (Auntie Ray) with nephew Tommy: 1916

THERE REALLY IS A 'WILLIAM'— BAD BOY OF THE BOOKS

By PAUL DEHN.

THE original of " William," scrubby, tousle-haired, inky-fingered little schoolboy immortalised by Richmal Crompton and subject of a new Elstree film with Dickie Lupino in the title-rôle, is now a twenty-three-years-old bank clerk working eight hours a day at a branch of the Westminster Bank in London.

THE REAL WILLIAM
—taken when he was ten.

But William is afraid that his identity will be discovered and that his staid and sober colleagues at the bank will mock him. So his name must remain a mystery.

He is Miss Richmal Crompton's nephew. Three things apart, he looks as mischievous to-day as twelve years ago, when he turned the hair of his elders and betters prematurely grey.

But to-day:

> There are no soup-stains on his collar.
> His hands are clean.
> His hair is brushed.

That's the price a boy has to pay for becoming a bank clerk!

At present he's working hard for a banking examination in a fortnight's time that may mean promotion and a rise.

But his interests are still mainly out of doors. He is a keen Rugger player, and has just joined the Territorial Army.

Miss Richmal Crompton told me that she was first inspired to write about him after the Ghastly Episode of the Stag-beetle and the Marmalade.

"He came home, one afternoon, with a stag-beetle," she said, "and hid it in the drawer that contained (as luck would have it) his under-clothes.

Bag Of Snails

"A day or two later he observed that the animal seemed to be ailing and, thinking that it was hungry, emptied a jar of marmalade—stolen from the larder—into the drawer.

"On the following morning he was delighted to see that all the marmalade had disappeared. In his innocence, he imagined that the stag-beetle had eaten it.

"But his mother subsequently discovered that it had soaked, beyond recall, into his underclothes !

"Things had a **knack** of disappearing with William," said Miss Crompton reminiscently. "There was the time he brought home a bag of live snails, and left them in the hall. After lunch, the bag was empty.

"His father discovered eleven of them on the dining-room mantelpiece. Six are still unaccounted for. . . ."

William's mother, who lives at Bromley, Kent, told me: "Every day he went off to school properly dressed, and every evening he came back with no laces in his boots and no garters on his stockings. He always said he had 'lost' them!

"I quite understood that the garters served as catapults, but I do not yet know what happened to the laces. Anyway, one pair of bootlaces and one pair of garters was part of our daily budget for William!"

March 5th

1939

Foreword

William Brown, irrepressible hero of *Just-William* and 37 subsequent books written by Richmal Crompton Lamburn, lives on long after his creator's death in 1969. Hardly a week passes without his name being mentioned with affection and amusement in radio or newspaper commentaries, keeping him firmly in place as a national institution.

It is estimated that by now more than 10 million copies of the William books have been sold worldwide. They have been translated into ten European and Scandinavian languages, also Hebrew, Czech, Icelandic, Gaelic, Afrikaans and several Indian dialects. They have also been published as school textbooks, with translation vocabularies, in Germany and The Netherlands.

As Richmal Crompton's eldest niece, now her oldest close surviving relative, I was intimately connected with William's development and progress from his earliest days. Richmal was my mother's younger sister; with only 17 months between them, they were devoted to each other throughout their lives, with the bond of shared friends, shared schooldays and mutual interests. They were separated when my mother Gwen moved to London from the family home in Lancashire and married Tom Disher; but a few months later Richmal and her mother moved south to join the Disher household, where they remained for several years before setting up their own home nearby. Eventually Richmal became a surrogate father for Gwen's family.

Many times over the years I have been asked to tell the story of the family in the early years when *Just-William* was gaining a hold on readers' hearts and minds, particularly during the Twenties and early Thirties – in fact the period between the two world wars. The ultimate seal of fame came with the making of the first William film in 1939. My story, never told before, concerns the childhood of the boy who was William's prototype: the boy who provided my Aunt Richmal with the opportunity of studying every facet of his character while she was writing the books. This was her nephew Tommy, an enterprising non-conformist – my late brother.

Media interviewers often expressed surprise at the way Richmal Crompton understood so completely the working of a small boy's mind: it seemed extraordinary because she had no children of her own, never having married. But it was not extraordinary at all. She had this small boy Tommy in front of her throughout the time she was developing the character of William. The plots in the 38 volumes of stories are an amalgamation of ideas, some written for Richmal by her own brother Jack when she needed extra stimulus. But wherever the plots came from, the *character* was Tommy – and the residents of Bromley (the London suburb where we lived) knew this well enough, sometimes to their amusement and often to their cost.

I was around when William was born but too young to appreciate his importance. We knew Aunt Richmal's stories about a small boy had started to be published in magazines and realised it was a sideline to her real work at that time of teaching at the local high school for girls. It was a great shock and tragedy for the family when she caught polio at the age of 32, and nearly died. Yet this was the event which led her to a full-time writing career that resulted in worldwide fame.

Meanwhile her nephew Tommy grew quickly into a lively, rough, tough boy, very accident-prone, always in trouble with neighbours and authorities, and involved in one difficulty after another. As he grew older and realised he was labelled Just William he denied the connection. For a young clerk in the Westminster Bank the label was embarrassing, and he always refused to be interviewed by the media.

When Aunt Richmal referred to incidents in her brother's early life, Jack Lamburn was no more pleased with the William label than his nephew Tommy. Jack had been very strictly brought up and maintained that he had had no freedom or opportunity to behave like William. In any case, Jack's character, although mischievous within the limits of his upbringing, was entirely different from William's.

In her own account in *Radio Times* in 1945 Richmal stated: ". . . a young nephew, much to my delight, if less to that of his parents, began in his earliest years to display the infinite capacity for producing chaos in his immediate surroundings, with the best intentions in the world, that is William's chief characteristic. Unlike William, however, he grew up and is now a respectable citizen, who – I believe – regards his reputation as an 'original William' with mixed feelings."

She spoke too soon. When she wrote that for *Radio Times*, Tommy was a private in the Army (having lost his one stripe soon after gaining it) and was later to have a rather chequered career in banking – hardly an appropriate job for a William character but, from his family's point of view, a safe haven. There continued to be a great many amusing incidents in his life, though he could never see why we were laughing. But they no longer provided suitable plots for the adventures of a fictional 11-year-old, so Aunt Richmal had to search for themes in other directions.

There were other family characters who influenced Aunt Richmal's writing, whose real-life adventures often formed the basis of William's aspirations. Adventure, even if only fencing with the local farmer's bull, was extremely important to William and his friends. In their dreams the Outlaws travelled the world, were pirates, bandits, showmen, dictators, Red Indian chiefs, parliamentary candidates and even saints. In reality Richmal's relatives did travel the world and sent reports of their adventures back to England. The two sides of the family – the Lamburns and the Dishers – showed plenty of enterprise from which Richmal could draw to enliven William's village life.

Much of the Lamburn family history has been told by Richmal Crompton's biographers but the story seen from the inside has never been revealed. For several years after my brother's death in 1983 I could not write about our youth, our relatives, the rather wild adventures and unconventional upbringing, and the adult years. Only now that some of the sadness has faded am I able to put this down on paper and recount the lighter side, which was frequently very funny and sometimes quite ironic.

Margaret Disher

I

Tommy in Trouble

As I opened the door of my flat that evening late in October 1983, I knew Tommy had gone. Among the pile of letters on the floor were two scrawled by hand, with URGENT underlined right across the envelope; both delivered personally in a desperate effort to find me. That could mean only one thing. I opened the first, from my niece.

"Tommy died at 10.45 this morning." The letter was dated Saturday October 22nd – I was a day too late. I would have come back earlier if the hospital report had not been so good. Three days before, when I phoned from Lugano, they had said he would be coming out of hospital this Saturday. It had been good bulletins all the way or I would not have gone to the vast textile machinery exhibition in Milan.

"Tommy died at 10.45 this morning." The words would not sink in. I could only think of the five hours' delay at Zürich airport, wasted time. But that made no difference really. It was still a day too late. The exhibition had closed on the Wednesday, much to my relief. Commuting between Lugano and Milan, then battling with the Metro, had become intolerable, especially as there was a strike of customs officers at the Swiss-Italian border, usually resulting in an hour's delay.

Three thousand of us were making this journey every day from Switzerland to Italy and back again because all Milan hotel rooms were full. We were the overflow, the outcasts. There were special buses directly to the fair grounds for exhibitors' staff, but I was merely a trade journalist, reporting the show. Three hundred and twenty journalists – the press office had gone mad, trying to churn out the latest progress reports in fourteen different languages.

Tommy dead. It was not possible. I felt a surge of anger because I had not been to see him in Bromley Hospital, only an hour or so from my flat in London. Before leaving England I had been torn between conflicting interests and had made the wrong decision. I had been in Manchester when Tommy had his first heart attack and returned to London determined to see him and (as next-of-kin) question

1

the hospital staff on the true situation. Unfortunately I had only three days in London to finish several articles before travelling to Zürich, then on to Milan.

During those three days – before I could get to Bromley Hospital – the purchasing officer of one of the USA's largest corporations had phoned, talking to me as if I were trying to sell him a substandard consignment of nuts and bolts. He wanted a formal "Proposition" so that the price for a lecture I had been asked to give to their staff could be authorised by his department. I was surprised. "But it's already arranged," I said. "The fee has been agreed by the only department concerned." However, he insisted that I must send a Proposition before he could issue a contract and I could not visit the company until that was done. "I will prepare it on my return from a trade fair in Italy. You will have it by early November," I said, trying to gain time. But he was angry at having his demands treated so lightly and insisted on my sending him the document straight away.

I considered cancelling my Italian work but the hospital reports were so good that I gave priority to the red-tape requirements of the Americans, which took longer than I thought. Having posted the Proposition, and by then running out of time, I dashed off to Italy, leaving Tommy in the care of friends.

Although the phoned reports on Tommy continued to be good while the Milan fair was in progress, between its closure on the Wednesday and the following Saturday, unknown to me, he had three more heart attacks and died. My air ticket had a fixed return date for the Sunday, giving me three days to spare; so, believing he was coming out of hospital, I had moved to the mountains above Lugano to recover from formaldehyde fumes, days spent trailing around exhibition halls and hours spent standing in the corridors of crowded Italian trains.

I tried to think what I had been doing at 10.45 on Saturday. I must have been in a long queue waiting to see a display of Russian-owned Impressionist paintings at the Villa Favorita. In my pocket were two beautiful large shiny conkers I had found while kicking around the fallen leaves in the wooded hills. It was many years since I had collected conkers for Tommy. He would be pleased and amused to have them. I had also bought him a small self-adhesive digital clock, smaller than a domino, that he could stick anywhere – on his face, if he liked. Now he would never see them.

My latest travel joke would have amused him. His sense of humour was not very subtle but he appreciated banana skins and own goals. My journey from Zürich to Italy had been ludicrous. After being lavishly entertained at Zug, a small Swiss town on the rail route south of Zürich, where I was to visit a factory, I was not feeling my best the next morning as I toured the plant. I suspect the technical director was also feeling off-colour but neither of us was prepared to admit it. When he finally saw me off at Zug station, to carry on south to Italy, he literally put me on the wrong train. Instead of a lake, which should have appeared half an hour later, once again I saw the outskirts of Zürich. There I missed the next train back again by seconds and had to wait an hour for another. As the train come into Zug – for my second time round, like Gerard Hoffnung with his barrel and basket of bricks – I saw it was at the same platform from which I had departed two hours before. I have since learned that the Swiss are not alone in having this dangerous system of using the same platform for trains in either direction, for British Rail have now copied the Swiss. If a train going south is late it is easy to get on the next train, on time, going in the opposite direction – that is, if you fail to hear or understand the announcements. I suppose in Zug we had been talking too intently. How Tommy would have laughed at that one.

But now I had to face facts down at Bromley Hospital. The day after my return I collected his personal possessions in a grey plastic bag, then the death certificate. I went through the same routine of registering his death and arranging the funeral that he and I had done together when our mother died, two years earlier.

The undertaker recognised Tommy's identity – the original Just-William, Richmal Crompton's nephew. "May I contact the local paper?" he asked. This was something I was anxious to prevent. "No. Please! Definitely not a word. He didn't like the connection. I can't let that happen at the end." The man nodded in sympathy and when the time came, only the family and close friends were there at the funeral. Not a word leaked out – except via the vicar's column a week later in the parish news-sheets, illustrated by a Thomas Henry drawing.

The fact that I never visited Tommy in hospital has tortured me ever since. Apparently he kept asking when I was due to return. Friends went in and found him fairly cheerful. ("You're really in the rough now," said a golfing partner.) After his death I questioned his doctor, who put the blame on excessive energetic sports when his heart was already tired. Then I remembered how often he had come in from golf absolutely exhausted, saying "I feel awful." He must have driven himself on, ignoring nature's warnings. We were taught to do that at boarding school. Unless we really exhausted ourselves, we were told, the games were not achieving their purpose. It was regarded as healthy to flog oneself nearly to death. That may be true for 16-year-olds but is not so good in one's 60s.

"It is incredible," people said, "Tommy dying now, at 68. Your family normally lives into their nineties." That was not quite true, for although my mother died at 91 and my father at 86, other members of the family had packed it in during their seventies. Aunt Richmal had died at 78, despite her ambition to reach 80. "I would only have to walk to the end of the road," she announced. "Then everyone would say, 'Isn't she marvellous!'" On the other hand she thought there was a lot to be said for dying, since one becomes an instant saint. Even worst enemies start saying how generous, kind and unselfish the deceased has been. Richmal's sense of the absurd was ever present.

Tommy had always looked so fit – rosy cheeks, bright eyes, thick curly hair, the picture of health except that he had recently put on weight. He had never smoked and only drank moderately. However, he did like food, just as William liked food. Tommy's second helpings were the same size as the first helpings and I always marvelled at the way he got outside huge platefuls of meat and two or three veg. Several years before my mother died he started to do the cooking, at first under her guidance. After a while I think they both became immune to the hazards of eating Chez Thomas, which was not always the case with visitors.

Over the next few months came the ordeal of clearing the house where the family had lived for 50 years. As Tommy's executor and trustee for the house, I had to make plans to sell the property. When I first went in, I found Tommy's laundry still hanging in the kitchen, pulled up to the ceiling on one of those bars with pulleys. Everything else was more or less in place. There had been no charwoman for at least a year; Tommy and cleaners never got on well. They used to move his possessions. "Someone has taken it" was his lifelong complaint and a cleaner was always suspect until he discovered the missing object at the back of a drawer or in his own pocket.

He must have been in pain and was probably up all that night I was in Manchester, when the first heart attack started. I expect he tried to phone my flat, possibly several times without success. I heard later from friends that he had tried to get a doctor during the night but was told he must wait till the morning and then an ambulance would come. I have no idea what he did alone during those hours of waiting and cannot really bear to think about it.

The house was, of course, cold and I did not understand the heating system. An estate agent friend living locally solved that problem, except that the time settings never coincided with my visits. I did not know the neighbours; they were different from my day. But an unofficial neighbourhood watch seemed to form itself to protect the house from vandals and squatters. I received phone calls in London from people I did not know, alerting me to problems, saying "The garage doors blew open in last night's gale. We have tried to tie them back with string." Whenever I turned up, a lone figure in cleaning clothes, it seemed that curtains twitched in nearby homes. This was suburbia at its kindest.

It was a sad experience, trying to sort out Tommy's possessions. He had not really cleared our mother's "personal effects", only her clothes. There were still the hair brushes, boxes of broken jewellery, watches, manicure sets and piles of small hemstitched and embroidered handkerchiefs.

Fortunately very few of Tommy's creepy-crawly friends were in the house – the insects he had loved in his youth. Some spiders had taken a fancy to his stamp collection, which was stored in a broken suitcase; he might, of course, have offered it to them as a home. Did they live on glue? Tommy seemed to have specialised in Colonial stamps of the Empire days; I saw the names of small states and islands no one mentions today, almost sunk without trace. My mind could hardly grasp the amount of administration the Empire must have needed, spread out so far without any quick communication . . . Only his sports gear remained; the other hobbies of his youth had been abandoned apart from chess – there were several sets with dog-eared boards.

I could have used professional house-clearers but felt it would be throwing Tommy's treasured possessions onto a rubbish heap for strangers to help themselves. I knew it was important to find a good home for every small thing. Fortunately a local old people's home needed furniture, bed linen, pictures, ornaments for a new extension – they had insufficient funds to buy such homely essentials for the new residents. Then a friend who helped with the homeless of South London immediately took the best of Tommy's shirts and underwear for needy men about to come out of hospital. I knew my mother and Tommy would have been pleased about that, because they supported a number of charities. A flood of appeals for funds carpeted the front entrance almost as quickly as I could pick them up. They had always had to be careful with money but it was an old custom that a set percentage of income had to be donated to a worthy good cause.

Friends came to help me on the odd days whenever I could manage a few hours at the house. A rather large collection of golf clubs, balls, shoes, tees, a trolley and umbrella had been left to a young neighbour just starting to play, which helped to get rid of much of the debris, as it seemed to me. I was interested to find a suitcase of photos stored on top of his wardrobe – mainly pictures of Tommy with girls. There were not many faces I knew among the more adult pictures. Like all brothers, he had been afraid of a sister's teasing tongue. There were photos of rugger teams, army mates, companions on walking holidays, seaside pictures and some official dinner at Grosvenor House, which was not really his scene.

I needed to find addresses for several recent girlfriends. Although he never married, the opposite sex remained a source of considerable interest to him, so there were letters. To read them would transgress the unwritten code of honour; but I did need to tell them that he had died, otherwise they would be hurt by an unexplained silence. I needed surnames and addresses. So I picked out the three latest and wrote to them, telling each one she had given him much happiness, which I am sure was true. His very last friend, Molly – the younger sister of his first serious love, Ruth – had helped me clear the house; she would take only his favourite chair and silver golf trophies as souvenirs, although I had offered her anything.

As always, many parts of the house were sticky – Tommy was a walking advertisement for honey and Ribena blackcurrant juice, and both had managed to work their way all over the house. In some places dust had settled on the tacky surface and formed a congealed layer. Although I had hired a strong man to go through the house, cleaning and removing obvious rubbish, in the end – the day before completion of the conveyance – I had to take a knife and cut away the sticky deposits and scrape Tommy's fingermarks off the sides of doors.

I sorted through the cutlery, which was mostly distorted and mis-shapen. Fork prongs splayed out at odd angles and knife blades fitted only loosely into their handles, ready to part company with their bent and broken ends. They had been used for various operations not specified in any cookery book. He had found that knives, forks and spoons were useful implements for emergencies with the lawn mower, wheelbarrow, bicycle, car, garden-shed door and all locks and bolts. He often gave up the effort after wrestling with these inanimate objects. The real handyman had been my mother, who just wished he would use the correct tools (admittedly rather rusty) which she kept in the spare room. The steady deterioration of our best cutlery upset her.

All the furniture had to be removed as quickly as possible. Some was sold, some sent to relatives and only the removal to the old people's home failed to go as planned. The van had been organised locally by their own staff for 10.30 on a Saturday morning. In the event, the helpers turned up but not the van and apparently several of them had other plans for the afternoon. After waiting an hour we took the only possible course, loading up two cars and strapping mattresses and bed frames to their roofs. We used the staircase as a chute, sending mattresses down from bedroom to hallways, counting in disbelief as thirteen came out of four rooms. The cars went there and back several times and then, when only the hall coatstand remained, the official van came sailing round the corner – two hours late. I was so glad to see it all go that I paid the one man the whole fee for moving the one item. Glad yet sad. I dared not really think about it. But all the time I had felt that Tommy was there, sliding downstairs on the mattresses.

One of the worst moments was when the local Boy Scout leader, an actuary in real life, came to collect the aluminium pots and pans. The saucepans had been in a roofless garden shed and unfortunately were full of dirty water from the six months' exposure. I had not thought to look for them until the moment of his arrival, which coincided with a thunderstorm. In torrential rain we pulled out the many pans, some dented and mis-shapen, and emptied them as the heavy rain streamed down our faces and clothes. I am sure he had imagined they would be presented to him all shining, clean and dry, beautifully packed. It was not so. And I had no idea why they had been taken into the garden in the first place.

It had seemed strange that there were no bottles of sherry. A half-empty bottle of brandy and a full bottle of wine, that was all. Apart from the beer he drank with his sporting friends, Tommy's staple diet was sherry. He liked a medium sherry; mother liked it dry. So they had separate supplies, mother being held down to a tight ration. At one time – when she was 90 – he found she was exceeding her quota in his absence, so he watered her sherry, letting me into the secret. During my next visit a week later she asked me to test her sherry. Trying not to laugh I took a sip and said, "Yes, there is something odd about it. It's more like wine. Can you complain to the wine merchants?" "No, I think Tommy's watered it," she insisted, which I knew was true. "Why don't you do the same to his?" I asked. She thought that a good idea and proceeded to operate on his bottle. We waited for him to return from golf and settle down to his evening drink. I watched his face and could see he knew he was stymied. Not a word was said by either of them as they drank their diluted sherries but an unspoken cease-fire was declared.

So it was with some surprise that I found no sherry. For my part I am prepared to drink it dry, medium or sweet and a bottle or two would have helped me on my way during those six months. But again, right at the end, I found it. Out in the garden coal bunker, left over from the bad old days and never demolished, was a load of junk put there by the strong man I had hired during the early days of the house clearance. There had been a lot of rain since. I could see the tip of an old ironing board sticking up, leaning against trays from a defunct refrigerator. Knowing this was my last unpleasant job after months of work on the house, I steeled myself and pulled everything out.

After the first few objets d'art were out on the lawn I saw my mother's old commode. On lifting the seat I found a long object wrapped in clean tissue which had survived the elements for so long. It was sherry – an unopened bottle. As I pulled it out I saw others, all neatly packed. I could hardly believe it: nine bottles! I lined them up in a row and laughed hysterically at Tommy's hiding place – not exactly a guarantee against watering. At that moment a neighbour peered over the fence to find the cause of such ribald mirth, so I handed her a bottle. Nine little bottles and now there were eight. After a few more visitors there were three, two, then one. In my moments of depression I could have done with those bottles. Why did he have to hide them that way? But even more puzzling was the thought of the strong man carrying the commode down the stairs from my mother's room. He must have wondered why it was so heavy.

Being alone in this house that I had never liked was quite an ordeal. Other houses I had loved, but not this one. To me it lacked personality and was boring, without charm; yet Tommy had loved it. My favourite was The Glebe, my aunt's house in Bromley Common just four miles away, where we had lived during the war. Another home I had loved was in Sundridge Park on the other side of Bromley. Memories of my birthplace in Denmark Hill were very vague but I could see from family photos that it had been a beautiful place, with character. The prize house, however, had been the one in Tahiti, with a roof made of plaited coconut tree leaves, raised up on poles several feet above the ground.

I knew Aunt Richmal had been sensitive to houses. They always played an important part in her books – especially in the family novels she wrote for adults. Among her titles were *The House, Leadon Hill, Abbot's End, Chedsy Place, Westover, Linden Rise* and so on. Many of her novels were based on places with personality, the scene of family dramas, sometimes through several generations. Our houses witnessed family dramas too. Perhaps that was why I disliked this house – to me it would always be the divorce house. Although I had welcomed my parents' divorce, there was still the memory of the worry and tensions and the financial problems when my father stopped all payments to my mother until eventually forced by the courts to pay the alimony, which was low enough anyway.

Most of her life Mother had provided a home for Tommy, except during the war years. I had moved to London in the late 1940s, yet Margaret's Room was always ready, awaiting her return, which was never more than a few days at a time. My much younger sister, born when Mother was on the verge of 40 and Tommy was nearly 14, had married and left Bromley. Tommy was now waited on hand and foot by a caring mother, which he liked. He was a tough guy and thought he was entitled to the freedom to pursue his many interests. Domestic chores were not for him. Just once, for no particular reason, he decided to make a cake and to everyone's astonishment it turned out a huge success. He lived on the fame and kudos of that one incident for a very long time.

For many years Mother did his laundry and every Saturday patiently removed the caked mud from his rugger shorts, sweatshirts, socks and boots, which I am sure few wives would have done. Then she would turn into nurse to deal with his fearsome bruises and patch up the cuts and gashes. It was always my private opinion that rugger was a game invented by men so that they could attack each other without the police being able to interfere. Tommy was mad enough to play until he was 52.

Up to the time Aunt Richmal died in 1969 I had gone home for Sunday afternoons whenever work permitted, about once a month. Normally I phoned Aunt Richmal to let her know and we both converged on the Bromley household at the same time. Her death left a huge gap in my mother's life. They had been devoted sisters all their lives. I have a letter written by Richmal, then ten, to my mother Gwen, aged twelve and already at boarding school. Richmal, always known as Ray in the family, ended her long letter in typically childish writing: "For goodness sake make the Cristmas holidays hurry up for I love you so. With love of loves, I remain your loving sister, Ray."

After my aunt died I went home every week and amongst other things did the mending. Tommy always thought his old underwear was immortal and only needed a stitch from time to time. It was amazing the way both my mother and Tommy managed to get seams unstitched, buttons ripped off, cuffs frayed, hems down and elbows worn through. In the empty house his clothes, except for underwear which had departed early, were almost the last to go, collected for charity sales; and I saw once again his strange plus eights, as I called them, which had been made by a local tailor – a caricature of plus fours. His best lounge suit had been too tight for many years but casual sports clothes had served him well, fitting comfortably like old friends, hiding his natural untidiness. He never bothered to fold polo necks; he used to leave them like concertinas, in a mass of small creases. His favourite trousers had the crutch halfway to the knees.

As Tommy grew older, a myth took root in Bromley that he had dedicated his life to the well-being of his elderly mother. It was, in fact, the other way round. When she reached 80, I pointed out that he should at least make his own bed. But imperceptibly, during her eighties, their roles became reversed. He retired early from the National Westminster Bank, in 1973, and eventually took over the household duties, which he knew nothing about. He relied on neighbours for help; they became used to his determined stride as he marched up to front doors and even back doors if there were no answer. He was invariably amazed that as late as 7.30 on a Sunday morning they were still in their pyjamas and not as friendly as he expected. His problems with a grandfather clock were legendary but I think neighbours were thankful he was unable to carry it from house to house seeking advice. Every nearby household became involved.

For the last five years of Gwen's life, Tommy looked after her like a mother. She had eyes only for him. All the time I sat with her while he played golf on Sunday afternoons she kept saying, "Where is Tommy?" Even when he was only in the next room she would ask the same question. That might have been a lifetime's habit, always nervous of what he was doing, but more likely at this stage she regarded him as her life-support system. There was also a bond between them that I could not share or even fathom. He was aggressively male, so there was no question of his being a mother's darling.

After Mother died I really believed that Tommy would start a new life, independent and free to do what he liked. He could play golf all day or travel to warm seas and sun-drenched beaches where he could swim or mess about in boats. I was sure he would find a kind young widow to marry, who would look after him. But he did none of these things. I offered to take him here and there but got the impression that he thought a sister would cramp his style when playing the field. The knowledge that he had only two more years might have made a difference but of course he did not have this knowledge. I thought his short-lived freedom very sad. He simply continued to live in the house alone.

When packing up all my mother's first editions of the William books, each one inscribed with a message from sister Ray, I found also the early Williams dedicated to Tommy and me. There were several shelves of the other books she wrote; and also books by Jack Lamburn, brother of Gwen and Richmal. Uncle Jack wrote under two names, John Lambourne and John Crompton. Although all these books had been bequeathed to me when Mother died in 1981, I had deliberately left them in place for fear of upsetting Tommy. What a pity the book jackets had been ripped off and thrown away. Looking at the books I realised that writing was our family disease, quite incurable. It was rampant on both sides of the family, so I had no chance of escape.

As for the Dishers, there were quite a number by Uncle Maurice, my father's younger and only brother, who wrote as M. Willson Disher. His line was biographies of famous stage names, also books on the circus and old music hall. Not to be left out, my father had written his autobiography but failed to find a willing publisher. Never one to let such problems impede his progress, he had selected a suitable publishing house and bought it. I took all the books away for safe keeping, the cartons almost filling a car.

My own writing was now suffering through constant interruptions. I was still trying to write features on the Italian trade fair, with deadlines every week or so, and at the same time prepare a lecture dossier to take with me on my projected visit to the USA. My mind kept wandering back to Tommy, the house, the insurance, Grant of Probate (which I had handled myself, not through solicitors) and the sale of the house. I had to pull myself back to the machinery brochures. *"A vital earthly to get our objectives is the development of high technology enterprises capable to compete in markets as competitive like high tech one is. Industries, institutions and the society are conscious of this, and they are making an effort not to loose this race. Advanced pour in this restlessness supporting their strategies in a good disposition of the conjecture, and syntonize perfectly in the collective idea of our international projection like a big challenge to the year 2000."* That was not my writing but a Spanish computer brochure. I pictured a rather desperate translator poring over the dictionary. He must have suffered the way I was suffering in trying to understand him – or her.

Tommy would have been hopelessly bored by machinery and computers but I had to battle on. It was all rather different from my first story, written at the age of nine, called "Betys Iventurs", later used by Aunt Richmal in one of her books. I seem to remember that Bety got rather involved with a snak and an uggly wich. I got no royalties. This was the first infringement of my copyright.

Tommy, Richmal and gardener at the Denmark Hill house

The old album of faded snapshots showed Tommy's progress from pram to scruffy small boy beside his first broken window. He was dark-haired in some shots, blond in others. In one snap Aunt Richmal, who was living with us in the Denmark Hill house, is trying to stop him hitting the gardener, or so it seems. In another Tommy and Aunt Richmal appear to be kissing Eskimo-style, nose to nose, as she holds him close – the beautiful child, pride and joy of the family. They had no idea at that stage what trouble he would cause.

I tucked the album under my arm, slammed the front door behind me for the last time and pushed the keys back through the letter box, as arranged. I had now completed the despatch of the boy who had done his best to get rid of me all those years ago.

II

The William Character

My earliest memory is of watching blood trickle from my head into a bowl and seeing the water change gradually from pale pink to dark red. Quite interesting, really. Grown-ups kept sponging my head while Tommy looked on with dismay at his handiwork. He had brought a broken flower-pot down on my head, pretending it was a hat, and was just as surprised at the result as I was. But it did make a mess of my dress. Years later I was told he had been punished by forced immersion in a very cold bath – the latest technique at that time in behavioural correction. Knowing Tommy, I expect he thoroughly enjoyed it except that – as he kept saying – he had not meant to hurt me.

The early photographs show an extraordinary degree of character in Tommy's face, right from his first efforts at standing alone, unaided – not exactly swaggering but fiercely independent and ready to go. Compare that with the bland and stupid face of me as a baby, two years younger. No wonder he planned to abandon me in the park. Assuming that Mother felt the same about the new baby, which had arrived in the house without warning, he tried to enlist her help but was hurt and surprised to find she wanted to keep it.

Mother, Tommy and the stupid new baby. 1917

14

Grown-ups were impossible to understand. The baby had no teeth, not much hair and its hands and feet didn't work. He also suspected that it leaked.

Finally his efforts failed and he was made to suffer the embarrassment of having the baby about the place, with Auntie and Granny also fussing over it. The baby lay in the pram, curling and uncurling its fingers, pretending to catch butterflies. It had to be helped even to sit up or lie down. It did not cry but made curious burps.

Up to this time Tommy had been the household's most important person. His very positive character was evident at an early age. His potential for mischief was plainly visible in photographs taken in 1916, when he was just over a year old: he sits in his pram, eager to get out and take part in the action. This was no ordinary child. Here was the supreme nonconformist and age was almost irrelevant. You can see the mischief brewing – the sense of adventure and enterprise too. This was the face that launched more than three dozen books. It is quite obviously the William character.

The face that launched 38 books. Tommy aged 12 months

Tommy, the eccentric individualist, was closely studied by Aunt Richmal, particularly while the first dozen books were being written and the William character formed. The spacious house in Denmark Hill, South London, was large enough for his parents, grandmother and Ray (as Aunt Richmal was called in the family) as well as Tommy and myself. It was Ray's home during her holidays from teaching

The house where Richmal lived with the Dishers. Denmark Hill

at St Elphins, the girls' school in Derbyshire, following her father's death in Bury early in 1915. Late in 1917, after obtaining a post teaching at Bromley High School for Girls, she found a small house for herself and her mother in Cherry Orchard Road, Bromley Common village, a rural area about four miles from the centre of Bromley town and not too far from Denmark Hill.

Tommy was four years old when the first William story was written, his age in the photo that shows such a guilty face beside "The first broken window", this time the greenhouse. It is all there – tough, scruffy, untidy, on the defensive because "it was not my fault". Another picture shows him, one sock up and one down, embarrassed by female company

– equally untidy, with knicker leg slipping downwards. His monkey-like ability to climb trees had a disastrous effect on his clothes.

The first broken window

Girls are so embarrassing!

Although it has sometimes been said that William's character was typical of all small boys, I doubt it. William and my brother Tommy shared an unusual character and both moved on a wavelength of minor disaster. There was no evil intent behind their actions; on the contrary, it was often while they were trying to be helpful that some baleful hand of fate would land them in an extremely awkward situation.

It was impossible to predict what my brother would do at any time because he rarely followed the accepted rules of behaviour. Convention meant nothing to him. "Tommy, you can't do that," had to be followed by an explanation, which was hardly ever accepted. As we tried to justify the reasons for society's rules he would knock them all down with a logic of his own, which left my mother feeling that the rules were, after all, rather silly. Personally I felt there was a lot to be said for some of his theories – particularly his insistence that too much washing made the skin wear out.

One of my earliest memories of Tommy logic is his theory that ducks on the village pond belonged to anyone clever enough to catch them. This applied to fish in the sea, so why not village ducks that had no owner? And when he arrived home with his quacking, struggling trophies it was impossible to make him understand why they had to be taken back to the pond. In those days there were similar misunderstandings about the ownership of "wild" apple trees, raspberry canes and cherries.

He would have looked after animals extremely well but my mother had her hands full already with the damage he caused to people and property and was tired of being confronted by furious neighbours. Although in the books William's dog Jumble caused few problems, our mother would not risk additional trouble.

Tommy always had to be different. At Dame school, while the rest of the class was being taught how to unfold like petals of a flower to appropriate music, he preferred to be an elephant, or a lion, moving on all fours. Any fierce animal would do to justify loud roars, which frightened the unfolding flowers. He was comparatively good when there was no ink or paint around, but all the same two schools asked my parents to remove him.

Worms, beetles and anything else that slithered or crawled interested him – particularly slugs and snails. Useful slimy trails were left, so he could see where they'd gone and put them back in his pocket. There was an unfortunate incident at a hotel in Falmouth when Tommy left his coat tidily in the cloakroom with his boots: several slugs found their way out of his pocket and other guests were later enraged to find trails of slime all over their hats and coats. We knew what to expect but other people became upset. My mother spent most of that holiday apologising to fellow guests.

When interviewed by the *Sunday Referee* in 1939 Aunt Richmal described the episode of Tommy and the Stag Beetle that gave her an idea for *Just-William*. "He came home one afternoon with a stag beetle," she said, "and hid it in the drawer that contained his underwear. A day or two later he observed that the insect seemed to be ailing and, thinking it was hungry, Tommy emptied a jar of marmalade – stolen from the larder – into the drawer, a bit more each day. He was delighted to see that all the marmalade disappeared. In his innocence he imaged that the stag beetle had eaten it. But his mother eventually discovered that it had soaked beyond recall into his underclothes and the stag beetle was dead."

Another of my aunt's favourite stories concerned a walk along a country lane when Tommy, having finished his share of some sweets, started – as always – to cadge mine. He threatened to lie down and die if I did not give him some but I kept on refusing. He then lay down in the lane and remained quite still. As my mother, aunt and I walked on and turned a bend in the road I looked back at the motionless figure, with tears streaming down my face, feeling responsible for my brother's death but still determined to keep my sweets. Immediately we were out of sight he jumped up and joined us, the whole episode forgotten; but I was upset and did not recover for several days.

My mother was calm and patient, anxious to put right anything that went wrong. And plenty did go wrong. At an early stage she learned to dread the appearance of neighbours bearing down on her with a stern and intent look. "Has anyone told you what Tommy has just done?" He broke windows, made holes in fences, trampled on flower beds when chasing aggressive dogs and cats, used full milk bottles in balancing acts (hoping to qualify for the circus) and with his bow and arrow shot through choice items of underwear hanging out to dry. He was no respecter of property. The only real but temporary damage he did me was with an arrow that cut my cheek, and the fairly deep cut on my head made with the broken flower-pot.

Naturally he was constantly pursued by the police, who would arrive breathless and exhausted at our door. They held him responsible for their deflated bicycle tyres and for broken shop windows. Market stall-holders would complain of his "heckling" during their sales patter. With all these complainants my mother was sympathetic and let them sit down to recover. She offered them cups of tea and developed a very good "helpless woman" act which eventually took over and possessed her completely. Tommy for his part maintained that the broken windows must have been incorrectly manufactured. Surely not even stupid grown-ups would seriously use whole areas of a substance that could not withstand an accidental encounter with a small stone! The stuff must have been badly made in the first place. Why blame him?

Frequent accidents dogged our lives: Tommy jammed between railings, his clothes impaled on fence spikes, torn by barbed wire and his person gashed and bleeding. My mother was quoted in the press as saying, "Every day he went off to school properly dressed and every evening he came back with no laces in his boots and no garters in his socks. He always said he had 'lost' them. I quite understand that the garters served as catapults but I never knew what happened to the laces. Anyway, one pair of bootlaces and one pair of garters were part of the daily budget."

In later years I hardly dared show my face in Bromley for fear of being reminded of our unconventional methods. A certain Mrs Dewhirst never forgot the day she answered the door to find the strange-looking boy and girl on her doorstep. I said, "Please could you mend my brother's trousers? He's torn them so many times this week we daren't go home." Trying not to laugh, or so she told me later, she took us in, debagged my brother and sent me into the garden to play with her daughter, about my own age. When the repairs were complete we went on our way without realising that Mrs Dewhirst was the wife of a well known military tailor with an establishment opposite Claridges Hotel in London. We could not have made a better choice.

Tommy was completely unselfconscious; he had very few inhibitions and was incapable of putting on an act, except to get my mother on his side before angry neighbours burst in on the family. Then he would conjure up an imaginary illness or encourage a genuine one for all it was worth. In fact as a child he had genuine bronchitis nearly every winter and once managed real pneumonia; he had badly grazed knees and legs, with countless bruises almost every week. Even a cold required pampering. Mother's sympathy and protection were his reward. He found health hazards so useful, particularly to get time off from work – to fit in extra golf sessions – that he developed a hypochondriac cult to full advantage. Yet his closest friends knew he was extremely tough, for all that.

However, his scorn for middle-aged illnesses was not even thinly disguised. The remark by a neighbour to my mother, "I'm a mass of nerves all the way up my back," remained a joke for many years. Mother's question, "Where does it hurt, darling?" was always met with, "All the way up my back." I suppose most families have these jokes, incomprehensible to outsiders. "I made it out of my head," was my mother's classic, referring to a meal we had just enjoyed. This naturally led to "Mother's head for lunch today." Her best Spoonerism was: "I'm going to make a tot of pee."

Honesty was a basic part of Tommy's character. He rarely told lies to get himself out of difficulties. He might exaggerate but he would not invent. Others might have called him tactless but by his own standard, if he expressed the truth, then it could not be wrong. He thought "white lies" were just as bad as black ones, so we got a frank reaction to the presents we gave him. In adult years he retained the same outlook; and however much we were accustomed to his honesty, it was still rather disconcerting to be told: "I'm sorry but I'm not the slightest bit interested in what you're saying." He would say it quite kindly, for he thought we ought to know; but it did tend to inhibit the flow of conversation.

Like William, Tommy was bored by a great many people and a great many subjects. Mother tried to make him listen to what others were saying, but it was useless when he was intent on some other project. Life presented him with problems and when frustrated in his efforts to solve them, he could be bad-tempered and rude. He was abnormally impatient, particularly when confronted with people he considered stupid, yet many of the difficulties in which he landed himself were due to his own stupidity. He had tunnel vision, looking neither to right nor left of any strongly held beliefs.

Although there was no trace of malice in his character, he did like to get revenge when it was justified. He was well intentioned and often tried to help people he liked against the injustices of life, usually with disastrous results. He wanted to expose the hypocrites and deflate the pompous and as he grew up he fought against most forms of authority. Yet he was always surprised when his mother was shocked by his actions. The last thing he wanted to do was embarrass her. To him the social conventions were meaningless, yet he realised that for some obscure reason she wanted him to conform. She need not have worried, for he was fairly well known in the neighbourhood and people made allowances for his eccentricity. I was a young observer of the fight to make him conform, sometimes taking his side, but more often trying to cover his tracks when I thought others would not understand.

In her biography of Richmal Crompton, *Just-Richmal*, Kay Williams points out the similarities between the William books and the Penrod stories by American writer Booth Tarkington, first published in 1914, and she quotes from both to illustrate the resemblance. It is doubtful, however, that a classical scholar in her mid-twenties, such as Richmal, just starting her first teaching job, would have spent time reading an American book of this type, to give her the idea of William as a character. And indeed Kay Williams, after analysing the similarities, concludes that they were almost certainly coincidental. She also points out that the two characters were in any case quite different, Penrod being at times cruel and dishonest, in fact an embryo villain, whereas William is full of good intentions and on the whole could be considered "kind"; which verdict might have surprised the Browns' neighbours and particularly his elder brother and sister.

Tommy was relieved to share the blame for William's escapades with Jack, Richmal's brother, whom she sometimes quoted as an early source of ideas. Tommy preferred to keep out of the limelight and, in order to avoid publicity, drew attention to the age gap between himself and William when the first book was published in 1922; he was seven to William's eleven. In fact the individual William stories had been published in magazines, before the first book appeared, which made the gap even greater.

In the first book – the only one called *Just-William* – the drawings show a boy younger than 11, whose feet hardly touch the floor when sitting in a comparatively low easy chair. There is a photograph of Tommy aged about six which is almost identical with those early illustrations; which makes

Tommy   William

me wonder whether Aunt Richmal had sent it to Thomas Henry, the artist. He was not the first artist to draw William but had been asked to replace another, whose interpretation had not appealed to Richmal. The first William story was published in 1919, earlier than the photo was taken; so that first artist's image of the boy was probably derived from galley proofs. Yet this could have been another case of coincidence. However over the years Thomas Henry imperceptibly changed the face of William, starting with curly hair but ending with short straight spikes and an exaggerated shape to the back of the head. Thomas Henry Fisher died in 1962 and the work was then taken over by Henry Ford.

Aunt Richmal, like so many authors, drew on her own experience of people round her. In the third of her more serious novels, *Anne Morrison*, she sketched a remarkable likeness of her father. In that and subsequent books several friends and acquaintances recognised themselves, and indeed some took offence. It is therefore not surprising that the young Tommy should have provided her with a model for William, although after a number of years William himself was to take over. He became very real to the whole family because in fact he was one of us.

Some of the William episodes are highly improbable, others easily believable. Some really did happen and scattered through the early books I can find the plots which relate to family or neighbourhood incidents that would have sparked off the ideas. Yet the real attraction of the stories lies in the way they are written – the humour is largely in the writing. Richmal had a superb sense of the ridiculous and her everyday conversation was littered with amusing observations of absurd people and situations. She always watched people, especially in public places like trains and restaurants, and noticed detail that we would never have spotted. Eventually we learned to identify "her" characters and would say to each other, "Auntie would like that one." Tommy himself was not interested; he thought the general run of people boring.

One of Tommy's colleagues at the National Westminster Bank, where he worked for most of his life, put his finger on the key point of Tommy's lifestyle, saying that he "needed an adventure a day". Since I share this thirst for adventure, I conclude it was inherited from our father. Indeed we were given an adventure a day in our youth, in our travels, even in our family dramas. This is also one of William's main characteristics. He sets out each day to find an adventure and we know at the start of each story he will find one, sometimes to his advantage but often to his disgrace.

The story of Tom Disher senior, Tommy's father, is important because it spotlights several characteristics which Tommy might have inherited, although they had completely different personalities. Did Tommy inherit from his father the extreme individualism, the complete disregard of customary behaviour, the creative initiative for which he was renowned, certainly in his younger days? All of these were part of the William character. And all these outside influences had their effect on Richmal's life and work.

Perhaps one could say that all children are like that; but how many carry these tendencies through into their 60s? Most are ultimately tamed by domestic responsibilities, financial worries, business problems. Although Tommy did become a little more staid when older he still managed, often accidentally, to become involved in a continuous series of happenings. How many men in their 60s have proposed to the same girl every day for weeks, taking an offering of a single flower, until the mother practically slams the door in his face? Ever optimistic, he thought each day would be The Day when she would say Yes. Life was still full of promise.

There was something of the underdog about Tommy and William, which has appeal. In my view Tommy never really found the right job or the right girl and it was very sad that he only lived for another two years after his mother's death, when – free of all responsibilities – he could have launched himself into any number of new adventures. It is impossible to imagine – convincingly – William married or with his own children or otherwise conforming to society's rules. One by one the Outlaws would have dropped away and married. They would have been replaced by other friends; but the lone figure of William would have remained, in later years still championing one cause after another, making blunders here and there, privately ashamed and apologetic because he hadn't meant things to go wrong.

Pre-polio days: Richmal the athlete, with me as ball-girl

25

III

Parental Odyssey

My mother was so frightened on her wedding day that they had to hold hot water bottles against her to stop the shivering while she was getting dressed. She told me years afterwards that this was due to the sudden realisation that she knew almost nothing about the man she was marrying.

She had become engaged to him in not much more than a month from their first meeting and the marriage took place less than two months later, in October 1914. In July she had answered an advertisement for a secretary in London. Having a BA degree in French, English and Maths and in addition a secretarial training including bookkeeping, she must have seemed to Thomas F. Rhodes Disher, then aged 27, the most appropriate of the applicants. At that time Mother was a nonsmoker and a total abstainer, both of which he had specified in the advertisement.

When she came to be interviewed on a day visit to London, he took her to tea with his parents and to a theatre before she caught the night train back to Bury. Then at the beginning of August, over the bank-holiday weekend, he travelled to Bury to meet her parents, staying the night and meeting various relatives including Richmal. At that time, all over the country, Army reservists were travelling to their depots, preparing for the start of war.

With the exception of Richmal, Tom was well received by the Lamburn family and shortly afterwards my mother started work in London, staying with a cousin. Only a few weeks later Tom sent a telegram to her father, the Rev. Edward Lamburn, requesting permission to marry, although Gwen was already 25 and needed no parental permission. It was a matter of courtesy.

What she learned several months after the wedding, almost by chance through her husband's cousin, was that Tom Disher had been a priest working in Newfoundland and Canada, although born in London, the son of a Civil Service accountant. Even as a schoolboy he had been very devout, going to school every day with a Bible tucked under his arm. For years he had taken part in children's and schoolboys'

Bible Classes, Christian Associations and Scripture Unions, and eventually decided to become ordained as a priest in the Congregational Church, which seemed the nearest to his own philosophy. He joined the Colonial Missionary Society and in 1907, at the age of 20, was sent as a minister to work in Newfoundland.

My father aged 17 and 27 – the man no woman could resist!

We were given to understand in the family that eventually he had resigned because he could not bring himself to baptise the child of unmarried parents; an ironical decision in view of his subsequent lifestyle. But his own account, written many years later, offered a different explanation. He declared he had found the competition and sectarian rivalry between the different denominations which had settlements there too aggressive – completely at odds with Christ's teachings. He did not wish to remain there, although he loved the country.

A few months short of his year's contract he had returned briefly to England, partly because it was possible at that time to cross the Atlantic for as little as thirty-five shillings, before going to Western Canada to take up a new appointment. As an interim job, he joined a sealing ship as medical officer to a couple of hundred crewmen for a two months' voyage. Sailing from St. John, Newfoundland, they located the areas that were swarming with seals, which they hunted for their pelts. They had various adventures resulting in narrow escapes, trying to cut through the vast icefields. His ship had to rescue the crews of other ships which had turned on their sides.

The new post in Western Canada took him away from the dramatic scenery of the icefields and huge icebergs, exchanging them for the farming areas of Manitoba and Saskatchewan. Even there it was 60°F below zero, colder than he had experienced in Newfoundland, and often he had to sleep fully dressed. While still a priest for the Colonial Missionary Society he also became a teacher, even headmaster of the town school at Herbert, near Swift Current, where he lived in a rather primitive way, but no more so than the local farmers. He was still holding services, generally in widely spaced settlements. He spent many cold nights studying the Bible and found he could no longer believe many aspects of the Christian religion. From then on he considered himself an atheist.

When my mother met him in 1914, he was in Wholesale Confectionery. His several warehouses were stocked with famous brands of chocolate, toffee, chewing gum, biscuits and so on. (There is no doubt that the Disher confectionery empire would have suited William extremely well.) As supplies became scarce during the war years, Tom added other warehouses for matches, stationery, toys, haberdashery and tinned foods such as fruit and sardines. Almost accidentally he bought a pickle and sauce manufacturing business (enter Mr. Bott!), which he ran for many decades. When in our teens we tried to keep track of his enterprises – which ranged through quarries, brush manufacturing, electric-light bulbs, curry powder and a printing works – it was almost impossible to keep up with what he was doing. Yet the real passion of his life was travel and his conducted-tour company, Per Mundum, gave him the excuse and opportunity to wander round the world.

After their marriage, Gwen and Tom first lived in a flat in Southeast London, where they were joined in the spring of 1915 by Clara, Gwen's mother, after the death of her husband Edward Lamburn from complications following pneumonia. Clara preferred to join her married daughter in London rather than stay alone in the Bury house. Richmal had by then left Royal Holloway College with a classics degree and accepted a post teaching at St Elphins, her old school in Derbyshire.

Tommy was born in July 1915, by which time Tom Disher had found a suitable house that would provide a home for all the family, including Richmal in the school holidays. No. 147 Denmark Hill stood at the foot of Champion Hill, opposite Ruskin Park, close to King's College Hospital. It had nineteen rooms and a large garden including a tennis court. To do everything in style he installed a cook, parlourmaid and gardener. He claimed that his dining room could seat 150 people if anyone wanted to hold political meetings, though according to my mother some would have had to hang from the light fittings!

Commentators on William have drawn attention to the Brown household, described in the earlier books as a rather well-to-do middle-class establishment serviced by cook, parlourmaid and gardener. In later books the live-in staff have disappeared and Mrs Brown, William's mother, presumably in a smaller house, has to be content with a daily charwoman. This was an echo of what happened to the Disher household.

I was born two years after Tommy and spent my first four years in the Denmark Hill house, still within easy reach of Granny Clara and Aunt Richmal, who in 1917 together moved to Bromley Common to be nearer to the local high school where Richmal was now teaching. They still visited Denmark Hill frequently and in turn we were often at Bromley Common, making excursions into the nearby countryside – a constant foursome of Mother and Auntie, Tommy and me.

By 1919 my father's business ventures had taken a dive downwards and he was looking for other outlets for his boundless initiative. The West Indies attracted him and he considered the possibility of developing their natural resources. So towards the end of that year he went to Barbados, Trinidad, British Guiana and all the small West Indies islands, then on to Bermuda. He sent back full accounts of his travels to my mother, saying that although he was having a wonderful time he had abandoned any idea of establishing a business in the area.

Having enjoyed the lifestyle and climate of the West Indies – such a contrast to the frozen wastes of the icefields – Tom Disher decided to visit tropical islands further afield, in the Pacific, with a view to settling there. He planned to form a colony by enlisting like-minded people to travel with him, and advertised for companions. He was pilloried by the press for this idea, which today would hardly raise an eyebrow.

In his plan no one would receive pay or make a profit. Each member of the colony would trade by barter but there would be a limit on the land that any one person could hold. He received replies from master mariners, doctors, dentists, engineers, school teachers and skilled technicians – just what he wanted. However, according to my father and confirmed by a press cutting I hold, the Foreign Office then issued a warning against the climate of the Pacific Islands, stating that it was unsuitable for Europeans. Although this was incorrect, the general publicity made him decide to go on his own and he refunded the deposits which some would-be "members" had already sent him. He went out via Canada and the USA and found Tahiti, in the Society Islands, everything he had imagined – beautiful scenery and a wonderful climate, populated by a friendly and attractive people.

Father stayed there the whole winter of 1920 and bought land in an area called Vaihihi, in the Papara district twenty miles from Papeete, the main town and port, and another small estate in Taravao, which is the narrowest part at the centre of the island's figure-eight formation. He spent most of his time in Vaihihi, growing vanilla, oranges, bananas and limes; he could get fresh meat from Papeete by delivery truck. Quite a number of European writers and painters lived in Tahiti, either on a short-term basis or intending to settle permanently. The spirit of Gaugin lived on. The majority of non-Tahitians were, of course, French and the natives spoke both languages, while Chinese traders owned most of the small shops.

In the spring of 1921 he returned to England, visiting first another island (Rarotonga), then New Zealand and Australia, where he travelled to most of the principal cities and interesting areas before finally embarking on a liner sailing to England via Ceylon, Port Said, Marseilles and Gibraltar.

By now his London business interests were recovering, so his main concern was the development of conducted tours. He realised now the war was over that touring parties overseas could be the opportunity he needed. Finding that none existed for Germany and Austria, he decided to make a reconnaissance tour of these countries. He set out for the

Rhine area then travelled throughout Germany, taking the Danube boat to Vienna where he stayed for two months. He planned to run personally escorted tours by rail, river and sea but by 1923 he had introduced some limited air travel.

All that is family history. But the other side of the story was different, for Granny Clara and especially Aunt Richmal, who had never liked Tom Disher, were furious at the way he left Gwen and his children for six months at a time, without providing adequate financial support. Richmal was in fact a very strong character, despite the impression she gave of being gentle and accommodating. I have seen her very, very angry and frequently this was caused by her brother-in-law Tom. I have no doubt at all that he was one of the main reasons for her removal to Bromley Common from the house at Denmark Hill in 1917.

By the summer of 1921 it had also become necessary for the Disher family to move out of the large house and into "rooms" in Bromley. Tommy and I went first to one local Dame school, where he frightened the little girls with his imitations of wild animals, then to another where the pupils were older. Aunt Richmal found Mother a teaching post at Bromley High School and then after a while located a small boarding school in the depths of Kent that would take Tommy and me, aged six and four. It was near enough to Bromley Common for frequent weekend visits while Mother was living with Richmal and Clara.

At the new school we learned to pay homage to the colours red and green and sing school songs. We dressed up as shepherds, lads and lasses for school plays but as usual

The lads and lasses at boarding school play:
Tommy and I, bottom row left

31

Tommy had trouble with the teachers. He was blamed for everything that went wrong with the plays and the singing, but in fact we had really discovered something important – that if several of us sang a low note when the others went up, the result was very pleasing. We may not have invented harmony but it saved us from boredom.

There was also trouble with Tommy's pillow in the boys' dormitory when he tried to make an Indian headdress. Having found some large goose feathers and slotted them into two garters joined together, he still wanted a lot more. So he made a small hole in his pillow and pulled out what he needed, discarding the smaller bits, but then had great difficulty in preventing a rush of feathers every time he put his head on the pillow at night. It was a little while before the staff realised they had to sew up the hole. Although it was not remotely like an Indian outfit, Tommy's pride in the result was worth all the fuss.

Our first lesson in gardening inspired some experiments which possibly led to Tommy's genuine interest later in life. We were shown how quickly cress would grow in a saucer merely in water. Having seen potatoes that were beginning to sprout, Tommy wanted real potato trees. Using some shoes he rarely wore, he filled the pair with earth and planted some potatoes he had managed to collect from the kitchen. No green shoots came up, even though he changed the earth; and eventually he realised sadly that cooked potatoes do not grow as well as raw ones – but not before a trail of wet earth had led the ever suspicious staff to his secret.

All this time we were unaware of a vital fact – that Mother had hidden us from our father. She had decided to separate from Tom and thought he would never find us hidden there in Kent. But he did. All I remember was suddenly seeing him coming towards us in the woods, when we were out for a walk with the others, escorted by a young teacher. He said he had brought us lovely presents and unwrapped mine first – a circular brooch with a small owl perched on a bar – and then Tommy's, a larger owl on a pin, like a badge. So, seduced by owls, we went quite happily with him and never saw any of the others again. The distraught teacher took her remaining charges quickly back to the school where the alarm was raised. They had no proof he was our father, but we had appeared to know him. The next day they had to pack our clothes and take them to Cherry Orchard Road. We had been kidnapped.

Father had almost immediately phoned our mother at the High School while she was teaching and said, "I've got the children and am taking them to Germany tomorrow. Are you coming?" She was powerless against this blackmail, although she considered that Germany in the spring of 1922 was quite unsuitable for young children. There had been sensational stories in the newspapers of black bread, no milk, no meat and all the other privations; but knowing her husband, she knew he meant what he said. For the sake of the children she would have to be with them. She agreed, obtained leave from the school and prepared for the journey, being reunited with us within two days.

By now Father was full of enthusiasm for Germany and Austria. Having paraded his flat feet and a minor rupture before the Army medical board, he had not been called up during the war, so was studying the German nation for the first time. He was very impressed and surprised that the cities and hotels were so scrupulously clean. It was also obvious that the Mark's steady decline in value would be to his advantage. He had advertised towards the end of 1921 and by now had several tour parties already arranged, so it had become necessary to appoint local couriers.

While Father made his base in Cologne, we stayed in Königswinter, a small town across the river from Bonn. It lies at the foot of the ruined Drachenfels castle perched on the top of a small mountain, accessible by donkey rides even today, alongside the modern funicular. For many years I held a vivid memory of the scene beside the jagged stone ruins with a long and steep drop to the river Rhine below. Old spreading trees shaded the tables of a terrace café where waitresses bustled in and out of the kitchens attached to a small hotel. From the viewing point one could see miles of the snake-like river dotted with barges and a range of hills disappearing into the distance. The high point was protected by railings which overlooked thick bushes and scrub growing on the rocks which went steeply down.

I had my sunshade open as we looked down on the river when suddenly Tommy's clumsy movement sent it spinning over and down. It settled on some bushes completely out of reach and no one could fetch it back. Forty years later I went back to have a look and found the whole scene exactly as I remembered it, down to the smallest detail; but there was no sunshade, no mother, no Tommy. Staying that night at the small Drachenfels Hotel, as the only guest in early May, was quite eerie. The next morning a mist enclosed the hotel and blotted out the spectacular view, and I regretted my choice. Yet later I was glad to have been there, because a year or two afterwards the whole terrace was rebuilt as a concrete monster with a huge enclosed observation area, restaurant and kiosks. I was told that the rocks had started to crumble and had to be reinforced. The semicircular concrete slab can now be seen from miles along the river.

Disher family portrait taken in Cologne 1922

In a way, that sunshade episode led to Tommy's falling into the Rhine. The scene was Cologne shortly afterwards, where a quayside led down to the water. He always maintained he'd seen my toy boat sailing out of reach and was making a gallant gesture to get it back before it was lost forever, like the sunshade. I happened to be looking at one of the large paddle-steamers and didn't see him fall. But I heard my mother scream and turned in time to see a quick-thinking skipper fishing him out again, very wet and rather frightened.

For our parents, the trip was not intended as a long one because of Mother's teaching. In other years she coached students from home but at this stage her work was full-time. Father went on to other cities in Germany and Austria, escorting the tourists while we went home. Mother spoke excellent French, which eased any travel problems at Ostend, and there were many times later when Tom tried unsuccessfully to persuade her to act as a courier.

The tours were advertised at low prices, offering sixteen days for less than £20, to include good-class hotels and all meals. He kept the parties down to 25, with two couriers. No payments were asked in advance, not even deposits. The tourists were met at Ostend and delivered back to the same spot. He collected payments in cash on the train between Ostend and Aachen (Aix-la-Chapelle), where he had finally established his headquarters, with a bodyguard of four young men to protect and bank the money. The tours generally went to Cologne, Mainz, Heidelberg, the Black Forest, Constance, Bregenz, Innsbruck, Zell am See, Salzburg and Vienna on the Danube steamer.

During another trip later in the summer we went on his second route – to Berlin. To our great dismay we were accompanied by an English governess as well as our parents, which was not at all to our liking. She was too strict and spoiled our fun. But Mother was popular with the tour parties and although she usually managed to avoid them so that she could go sightseeing on her own, she did have to be polite; and the governess gave her more free time.

Tommy was thinking hard about how to get rid of our jailer without too much disgrace, to get our mother back again. In the end an opportunity came accidentally. We were in the wooded park on the outskirts of Berlin where we found a Y-shaped tree branch and from the rear got the governess firmly wedged with her waist in the fork. Then we could push her along the path. She managed to release herself but was so embarrassed to see everyone else laughing and probably also amused by our determined and serious expressions, that she gave notice immediately she saw our parents again. She stayed on for a while, however, as my father's guest.

By then the jailer had managed to teach me to count in German. I sang my song "Ine swy dry fear . . .", but Tommy was not interested. He was quite prepared to leave German to the Germans. He was busy carrying out his first industrial experiment: making chocolate balls. He was hand-moulding flat chocolate into a more interesting shape. The process, including testing, dispensed the surplus onto his hands and face. He decided the chocolate balls needed to harden, so he put them out on the windowsill to dry in the sun. A few hours later he was confronted with the failure of his experiment (especially disappointing because of the scarcity of chocolate) and had to retrieve what he could with a spoon.

We flew for the first time from Berlin to Nuremberg, a city my father thought the most beautiful in the world; but although Tommy and I thought the city walls and towers were marvellous, we were too young to appreciate the rest of it. The same could be said for much of our European travel. We were dragged round museums and thought them a bore. Yet I absorbed the atmosphere of many different places and cultures which could be picked up again when, as an adult, I retraced our steps quite accidentally through work connections.

The plane to Nuremberg had a small passenger cabin rather like a helicopter's – it was a flying taxi. But we had only gone a short way when Tommy was sick all over my mother's fur coat. I am sure I remember correctly that they wound down the window, as in a car; and the newspaper used to clean up the coat and upholstery was dropped overboard. I remember wondering about the farmer below who might be at the receiving end. My next flight was not for another 22 years, and then by courtesy of the RAF.

My father was charged a million Marks for the cleaning of the plane but, owning to depreciation at the time, this cost him only a sterling shilling or two – five to ten pence in today's currency. He banked minimum stocks of German currency, keeping his main working capital in sterling and only changing it for day-to-day needs. A full meal of several courses cost sixpence and a generous tip came to one penny. Eventually this situation went into reverse with the Reichsmark's introduction. As the cost of hotels and fares became more expensive, the Per Mundum tours were extended to France and Spain and even world tours, covering the Indian continent and the Far East and lasting up to seven months.

Our travels that July and August had led us from Cologne to Hanover, Berlin, Nuremberg, Regensburg and Vienna where we stayed for several weeks. We wandered through the Schönbrunn Palace and the Hofburg but there were no Spanish horses and no Vienna Boys' Choir. In due course tourism would bring them back. We were the vanguard.

However, the Volksprater funfair and gardens were in full swing, with the Big Wheel revolving daily. It became more of a landmark for Vienna than anything else there. The huge switchback frightened me into wild screams as it started the rush downhill; I have hated them ever since. St Stephen's Cathedral seemed small in comparison with Cologne's Dom. What we loved most about Vienna were the narrow alleys and coffee houses and the musicians – who no longer play in the streets. Yet in a way it was a rather sad city, licking its wounds, for the total depreciation of Austrian Kronen had ruined many people and they could no longer afford the upkeep of their homes. This cause was something we did not understand at the time, of course. And we were equally unaware of the Austrian Empire's history, despite Mother's attempts to explain.

The river held endless fascination, with so many ships and barges. Seen from the heights of the Vienna Woods it looked blue some days, but at quayside level it was always grey. Vienna was a much more attractive place than Cologne and I nursed a secret passion for my father's Austrian courier.

The train journeys were endless. We returned through Innsbruck and Switzerland, then back to the Hotel Lorelei in Königswinter, our base. Somewhere nearby we picked blackcurrants at a special farm and were allowed to eat everything we picked. In a fit of bravado I opted to stay the night at the farm. In an attic room I secretly cried for my mother, who thankfully collected me the next day. I pretended it had all been a great treat.

When we returned to Bromley, Aunt Richmal wanted to know every detail of our travels. She was always at the receiving end of other people's stories of adventure, which she greatly enjoyed. Her brother Jack was in China following six years in Africa and had given graphic accounts of his life and work when on leave and in letters. But she found Tom Disher's personal travelogues too egocentric, as if he had a desperate need for admiration.

Towards the end of 1922 Mother left her teaching job to prepare for our departure for Tahiti. It was to be a long absence from England. We were thrilled to have six weeks on a huge liner going to Australia and pleased to find other children on board. But people always pointed accusingly at

Tommy when waiters carrying trays along the deck suddenly dropped everything with a crash, to the sound of scurrying feet and slammed doors. It was not always Tommy's fault but as he and the purser appeared to be sworn enemies, proving his innocence was difficult.

For instance, he was accused of committing a nuisance into a colonel's boots put outside his cabin door for cleaning. Tommy denied the crime emphatically and we, as his family, knew it was not his style of conduct. We also knew he did not tell lies if guilty. He would make a million excuses and project his own reasoning but would never deny what he had done. So we knew some other boy – or a drunken man – must have done the job. No girl could have had such an accurate aim.

Mother found the ship had a claustrophobic atmosphere, which to her made six weeks seem a long time. Like Tommy, her husband cared little about social conventions and made frequent faux pas by her standards. He did not care whether asparagus should be eaten with the fingers. It was ridiculous, he said, when suitable implements were available, for him to get his fingers wet and greasy, with water running into his shirt cuff. Fingers were fine in Tahiti but not in the ship's dining room. Personally I agree – when alone I use a knife and fork and despise myself for complying in public with a very stupid custom. But Mother suffered contemptuous glances from fellow passengers who tried to make him look ignorant. They had no understanding of such a strong independent character. The truth was that he played bridge every night and won heavily, and that never makes a man popular. Also he told a lot of schoolboy jokes and sprinkled his conversation with puns.

The ship's shop was our paradise, the only problem being that nothing was free. Fruit in the dining room was free but immediately one went through the doors money was required for exactly the same fruit. There were small bottles of sweets for sale and packets of chocolate-coated raisins. Tommy noticed that I did rather well, receiving daily presents. I was overheard giving him advice on how to acquire these goodies: "You should be nice to the men."

In the children's special dining-room we held competitions to see who could balance the most plates on top of a cup, then lift the cup without touching the plates. The knack was to turn the cup upside down at the start, then not so many plates got smashed. We were able to blame the slight roll of the ship.

Tommy managed to spirit fruit from the dining room into our cabin. He had decided that fruit could be used as currency once we reached Tahiti, for trade with the natives. He had heard stories about beads but thought fruit was better. The only hiding place he could find was an empty suitcase, so the hoard grew without his noticing that the fruit had lost its youth. Eventually, my father discovered the rotting fruit and the whole suitcase had to be washed and disinfected.

We called in at Gibraltar but I remember nothing of that. Perhaps the town was too much like England to make an impression – no strange people and no strange smells. At Port Said the sharks swimming round the ship left a lasting picture in my mind – of long black shapes gliding through the water.

There was a big drama in Colombo when we left the ship for a day. Lined up outside the Customs House was a row of rickshaws. Tommy and I were helped into one by a little dark man; there was just room for the two of us sitting side by side. The man took his place between the shafts and Tommy shouted "gee up" as if he were a horse. The rickshaw set off at high speed while I stood up and screamed. The man was running off with us into a hot dangerous place, away from our parents. After some commotion our "horse" stopped and looked for the second rickshaw, which he thought was following. I screamed and cried until our parents caught up, wondering what murderous attempts had been made on our lives. As always, Tommy got the blame.

Many years later, in the 1980s, I had some work assigned to me in Colombo. Managing to avoid the obvious modern hotels – like the Intercontinental or the beautiful Oberoi – I stayed at an old colonial-style building which used to be the Grand Orient Hotel. Its restaurant is on the fourth floor, with a wonderful view right over the harbour. There was just one old decrepit rickshaw left, with a little man offering rides. Today rickshaws have been replaced by small motorised rickshaw taxis, three-wheelers forming an exclosed cabin for two. In the end I was drawn like a magnet to the old rickshaw to look for the same quay and Customs House that had been there in 1922.

It was still there, up the side of the harbour. We then made a tour of the nearby seafront, which is laid out so like a British seaside resort with grass and promenade that I almost looked for the pier. It was hot, so the rickshaw man and I sat a while on the grass and looked at the sea – not at all what would have been done in the days gone by. The rickshaw was as much a curiosity to the youth of Colombo taking their Sunday stroll, as it was to me. I paid the little man what would have been a Sri Lankan's month's wages and sent him home. He would never know why I gave him so much. He probably thought I did not know the value of the notes.

The atmosphere of Colombo and even Kandy was familiar to me: the heat, the dilapidated dusty buildings, the narrow pavements and uneven steps, the craftsmen's workshops, the temples and the smell of jasmine – so many things. And yet I had only been there before for the inside of a day. The harbour was now empty of liners and excited travellers, with all their luggage. It seemed deserted, with only a cargo ship here and there.

Travelling by air now, people miss out on the big event of a liner: crossing the line – the Equator. This is an important ceremony. Father Neptune makes his appearance and passengers, mostly volunteers but not always so, take a ducking. As I was only five and a half at the time I cannot remember the exact procedure but I can still see a canvas pool being constructed and filled with a ghastly mixture of lemonade, fruit (Tommy's rotting stock had not yet been discovered), shaving-soap bubbles, tinned milk and all manner of things that did not normally mix. The sight inspired Tommy to contribute whatever else he could find. He dashed excitedly to and fro, pouring things into the pool, aided and abetted by the ship's crew. He was one of the first into the pool, in his underwear, and came out grinning in between fits of spluttering and coughing. Quite a few people joined in the fun but I was content to watch from a distance, fearful of being pushed or pulled into the sticky mess.

We spent a week in Australia before catching another ship to Tahiti – this one much smaller, offering no escape from officious grown-ups. The crew were more friendly and explained how things worked and even helped us climb into lifeboats to play pirates and shipwrecks, which was very soon stopped by the captain. He said Tommy was wild.

Photo: A. Sylvain

Tahiti, on the other hand, seemed to have a civilising effect on Tommy. It was only a matter of relativity because there were fewer restrictions, rules, social customs, shibboleths. He felt really at home there, just as my father did. Apart from the wonderful climate and scenery, Tahiti meant liberation to Tommy. He was able to be himself within the easygoing atmosphere, where everything was informal. He did not have to be clean all the time; though even that did not prevent his open envy of the Tahitian children's brown-tinted skins, which provided a natural camouflage for dirt. He did not have to keep to time schedules. The only rule was to wear a sun-hat and sandals.

To wander in the sunshine with practically no clothes on would be any boy's dream. Tommy was fascinated by the vivid blue lagoon and the brilliantly coloured fish, which could be seen at their best by dropping a few feet below the water's surface. The sandy shore had coconut palm trees growing right down to the water's edge, and the hermit crabs scuttled into their holes round the tree roots as soon as we approached. They were so nearly caught yet always escaped at the last second.

A stream from the mountains splashed over small boulders down to the sea, with a plentiful supply of small prawns and fishes nestling under the stones. The stream served for washing, drinking, cooking water and general cleaning until my mother found there was a VD colony higher up on the mountain. Then Tommy and I were told the stream was out of bounds because some sick people were washing there. The other hazard was the poisonous sea urchins, which hid just below the surface of the sand; they were one of the main reasons for sandals. Fortunately the place was comparatively free of snakes and we were not bothered by mosquitoes.

Tommy's old barn – Tahiti

(below)
Tommy and I with builders outside our main house – Tahiti

Our two houses were built with roofs of plaited coconut palm leaves and raised about six feet above the ground, on poles like stilts. One was for family living quarters and the other a daytime house for Tommy. Why he had a house to himself I do not know and never thought to ask. He was immensely proud of it, like William with his barn. No doubt my father used it as an office in the following years. There were also sheds for our hens and the horse that used to take us by cart into the capital Papeete, twenty miles away. Mother bought large quantities of rice there from the Chinese shops, hoping it would be wrapped in French newspapers – her only original source of international news. Our parents could get duplicated newssheets of brief items received by radio in Papeete; but as far as Tommy and I were concerned, the outside world did not exist.

Our "helpers" on the land my father had bought were our neighbours Fifi and Nani, husband and wife. Fifi assisted my father with his plantations of vanilla and oranges while Nani helped with housework. As they only worked in the mornings, Nani returned in the afternoons as a visitor and my mother was obliged to entertain her as a guest. She brought us a present every day, generally a few cooked bananas, which we loathed. Fresh bananas were always welcome; in fact we used to pick bunches off the trees and share them with the horse. Yet when cooked, they have a very different taste. Tommy was ordered and almost bribed into silence on the subject, for we could not let him tell the truth; then we buried the bananas in the sand when she had gone. When the time came for Nani to move the oven, which consisted of a few bricks sunk into sand, to our horror she selected a new site exactly where we had placed her most recent gift.

Most of the time the temperature was very warm yet not too hot; there were occasional storms and high winds when coconuts blew off the trees and fell like bombs, sometimes crashing through our rather flimsy roof. We had iron bedsteads with strong metal mesh and springs which provided good protection. We were made to crawl underneath once a storm had started, whatever the time of day or night. Many years later a small hurricane touched the area and a rare tidal wave washed away both our houses. They were too close to the sea.

Coconuts were very desirable yet out of reach. We watched

with envy the Tahitian boys as they skimmed up the trees at great speed and Tommy spent hours trying to learn the knack. He had been a good climber back in England but nothing compared with these little boys. He could never get more than halfway up and his progress was slow. Coconuts proved a good source of liquid refreshment after the stream was put out of bounds. We learned to make a hole and drain the juice, then open it and make white coconut milk from the flesh. Otherwise my mother would boil the stream water on a camp fire. This was a long, long way from our life at Bromley Common and we had many adventures that William would have loved.

PAGE THREE. Naughty! I should have worn a hat.
Shrimping in the river at Papenoo, Tahiti

Tommy was in his element, spending most of his time catching the small beautifully coloured fish in the lagoon, which became our staple diet. These really were wild. He was a very good swimmer and tried to see how far he could go underwater, deliberately giving my mother an occasional fright by swimming in his straw hat, then shouting and lifting his arms in the air before disappearing, leaving his hat floating. The first two or three times my mother thought a shark must have got into the lagoon (which was protected by a substantial coral reef) and caught Tommy. But once she had started a rescue alert, he would surface some distance away. At that stage I could not swim so simply watched in admiration.

Tommy, gone native, nursing a sick Tahitian chicken

The only native Tahitian feast we attended was a tribal celebration and the guests all seemed reasonably happy before it started. We were not to know that their bonhomie was due to a local brew. Since all women and children were made to leave before the feast got under way, I never saw the finale; but I remember seeing the food laid out on cloths spread along the ground, with pieces of meat and fish on large platters with bowls of different sauces. The meat was usually taken in the fingers, dipped into a sauce and eaten rather noisily.

The Tahitians often fished at dawn, starting out in the dark in their outrigger canoes. Occasionally, as a special treat, we were allowed to go with them. In Papeete we watched the pearl-divers for hours on end, hoping they would come up with the rare black pearls. In those early days the town was primitive compared with today's evident sophistication and tourist amenities. There were beaded curtains for shop doorways, open quayside markets, rickety buses, people sitting on the verandas of wooden houses and beachcombers' cafés and bars round the small harbour, which was large enough to take the small cargo and passenger ships from Australia, New Zealand and San Francisco, which came about once a month. There would be no planes for many years yet.

The girls and women wore printed cloths, and some with interwoven designs, called pareus, simply wrapped round from armpits to knees with the ends tucked into the top. Unwrapped, the pareus resembled a tablecloth and we brought several back home to use that way. For festive occasions the girls wore neck garlands and flowers in their hair. Today grass skirts and all manner of fancy headdress decorations make an appearance to entertain the tourists, Papeete being a new playground for the rich, with expensive yachts in the harbour.

Yet nothing could spoil the beautiful sunset. Many artists, from Gaugin to modern painters, tried to recreate it on canvas but made the colours so brilliant that they were not believed. Many years later when my parents divorced I secretly commandeered one of the many watercolours my father had bought from Alastair MacDonald, a painter living and working in Tahiti in my father's time. It looks like an imaginary scene, with so many colours streaked across the sky; yet it was true. I saw it night after night.

Moorea, another volcanic island, a 12-mile hour-long ferry-ride from Tahiti's mainland, seemed greener, partly because it has deep valleys covered with lush tropical vegetation. Both islands have sharp mountain peaks, one of Tahiti's being 7,000 feet high. We loved the dramatic wide river at Papenoo, the other side of Papeete, where the fish were plentiful and the water colder. Tahiti is the largest of the islands of French Polynesia, also known as the Society Isles, and it covers 400 square miles.

Father had already spent two winters in Tahiti before we went there. For a while after we first joined him Mother sensed a coldness from the local Tahitian families and eventually she realised the reason. It had evidently been tactless of him to bring his European wife and children to the island. She gained an impression that he had been friendly with a Chieftain's daughter and my mother was therefore resented. The Tahitians believed that an actual marriage ceremony was not necessary: if a man and woman lived together, that in itself was a bond. In fact the man merely moved into his wife's parents' household if the father approved – the reverse of the Asian system.

Mother was, in fact, quite glad to start out for England. We travelled back through the USA, arriving in San Francisco in the early summer of 1923. We stayed there for a short while. My father always told a tale of my "getting lost" in the city when, on the contrary, I found my way back to our hotel through very wide streets with busy traffic for a distance of more than a mile. Always we were taught the name of our hotel whenever we travelled, and if possible the address. I had quite simply asked people for directions; which could have tragic results today, but at that time it was reasonably safe. I was going up and down in the lift, learning from the lift boy how to operate the controls, when I saw Tommy, my parents and a number of uniformed police coming into the hotel. I wondered fearfully what Tommy had done. But for once the police were looking for me.

Instead of the planned train journey, my father decided to drive us across the States. He had previously only driven a side-car motorbike, so agreed to take a half-hour lesson at the wheel of the car. He bought the car, several crates of oranges and food before we set out, first for Los Angeles and then for the Mojave Desert. The oranges were intended for thirst-quenchers because all the water we could carry would be needed for the car. I remember the wire mesh tracks laid over the sand to indicate and stabilise the route. Railway lines crossed part of the desert and it was said that cars could stop the trains to ask for water, but no train ever came our way. Tommy and I would have enjoyed that experience but there was only one a day.

Our next most important sight was the Grand Canyon. Mother took some snap-shots but unfortunately they failed to show the vastness of the place and its immense depth, which was said to be a whole mile. I could not see the bottom or even imagine that depth. Our next famous sight was the Petrified Forest, mostly tree stumps turned to rock. What appealed most to Tommy was our adventure near the Rio Grande river, past Santa Fe, when trying to ford a smaller river our car became wedged in the sand. Indians working nearby pulled us out again. For the whole of that day Tommy kept asking, "Were they *real* Indians?" He could not accept the absence of feathered headgear but was excited by the adventure.

Many things happened to our car, all along the route, especially as we travelled up and over some of the highest and most dangerous passes of the Rockies. We ran out of money through unexpected costs of frequent car repairs. Sometimes we slept in the car when Father drove us through the night. We had reservations on a ship from Montreal to England so time had begun to worry him. Cash would be available, he always said, at the next town – if only we could get there. Mother offered her rings as deposit at one of the banks. Our route took us through Kansas City, St. Louis, the outskirts of Chicago, Cleveland, Buffalo and so on to the Niagara Falls, another sight we could hardly believe. To Tommy's delight we collected a tortoise on the way, near Kansas City. We found him in the middle of the road, named him Jimmy and took him back to Bromley, where he lived for several years.

On finally reaching Montreal, we were all exhausted. When travelling at night Tommy and I had taken turns in lying on the back seat. The other would take the floor. When it was my night on the floor Tommy used to land on top of me every time there was an accident. I preferred to have the seat and land on him every time the car ran off the road, into a ditch or down an embankment, stopping suddenly. At other times car parts were torn and a wheel was smashed; even the steering rod became bent. So there was a thrill in having a hotel bed for two days in Montreal – and some money. We went shopping in a large store and as the others got out of the lift I slid down onto the floor, exhausted. A few minutes passed before I was noticed by passengers getting in at another department and by then my parents had started the alarm. I was taken to our hotel apparently unconscious. A doctor pronounced that, as far as he could see, I had no specific illness but should not be moved for two or three days.

This meant missing the ship and Father was furious. He wanted me left in Montreal, to be forwarded on the next ship like a piece of luggage. Mother refused to leave me, alone and – in her view – ill, in a foreign country where they often deliberately refused to speak or understand English. For once Father was beaten, and so we stayed until I was fully awake and recovered. The ship we had meant to catch hit an iceberg, so on the next one a week later, we had to call at St. John, Newfoundland – Father's old base in his days as a priest – to pick up passengers who, though still rather shocked by this experience, wanted to continue their ill-fated journey. Within my family I was, in the end, a popular girl.

We recounted to fellow passengers all our car accidents and with great pride listed the States we had travelled through – California, Arizona, New Mexico, Colorado, Kansas, Missouri, Illinois, Indiana, Michigan, Ohio, Pennsylvania, New York State and so on to Canada. Yet it was only twelve out of forty-eight. Even in adult life, through four more visits, I only managed to add four more States – Delaware, Tennessee, Georgia and Louisiana.

On reaching Bromley, our first thought was to tell Aunt Richmal and Granny every detail of our travels. We knew they had gone to Cromer on holiday but would be back by now. We could hardly wait to dazzle them with our accounts of adventure in the tropical seas and the vast continent of the USA. So Mother, Tommy and I went immediately to Bromley Common to give them a surprise. We banged the knocker of the Cherry Orchard Road house. Instead of letting us in, Granny came out, shutting the door behind her. She shooed us away while she and Mother had a low murmured conversation. They looked so worried that we could guess something dreadful had happened. Where was Auntie Ray?

IV

Portrait of a Family

Aunt Richmal was very seriously ill. They had been obliged to return from Cromer after only one week because the hotel refused to keep her: a local doctor had diagnosed polio and she was highly infectious. After a nightmare journey Clara had got Richmal back to Bromley Common and for more than a week no one knew whether she would live or die. Clara nursed her almost night and day continuously. Mother did what she could, buying food and medicines, but she was still barred from entering the house. She waited anxiously for bulletins each time the doctor called. In the daytime we were left with friends in Bromley, both Tommy and I subdued by the calamity. We had not realised that grown-ups could be ill. We could not understand how Auntie, who was to us quite old – in fact 32 – could get something called infantile paralysis.

After the infectious stage was over, we were allowed to see her for a short while almost every day. She liked Jimmy the tortoise but thought he must be very old, having so many wrinkles. We carried him with his lower half tied up in a paper bag to avoid getting our clothes in a mess without warning. Granny was quite particular. We saved bits of food from our meals to see if he would like them but Jimmy seemed perfectly happy with lettuce leaves.

Our travel stories were rather incoherent so Mother was the one to give a full account. Every now and then she lowered her voice so that it was impossible for us to hear; but we did catch the word "Tom", so knew it must be about Father. We showed Auntie some of the snapshots of Tahiti which were quite good but we had no pictures of the P & O ship or Australia. There was one of Tommy and me with absolutely nothing on.

Aunt Richmal went by taxi every few days for various hospital treatments, some of them said to be "electric". Her right side was paralysed but the use of her hand and arm gradually came back. We helped her do exercises to get the muscles working and were thrilled when she could once again hold a pen and write. She kept assuring us that as long as one finger was working she would be able to type, although we knew that most of her writing was typed by someone else. In the end her right arm worked just as well as the left, yet it seemed that nothing much could be done for her leg. For a long while she had to use crutches, then she graduated to two sticks and eventually to one, but she was to drag her leg for the rest of her life. She used to make jokes about it, and never complained.

After a while Richmal started to write again, working hard behind a closed study door, and so we spent more time with Clara, who was very strict about punctuality. Everything depended on the clock; when she said "one o'clock" we knew she meant ten to one o'clock, then wash your hands and comb your hair. This was Clara's only disadvantage, set against her many good qualities. She was majestic, beautiful, kind and sympathetic – though not actually cuddly, like Mother and Auntie. She was humorous, yet not in the same way as Richmal, who liked odd people and funny situations. Clara ran the household very efficiently, as she had done in Bury, but now she had to do the cooking herself. Her speciality was the most marvellous treacle toffee.

Left in peace to concentrate, Richmal started to write short stories for *Punch*, *The Humorist* and *London Opinion*. She had been secretly writing short stories, including William, during the time she was teaching at the high school. This was against the terms of employment but when the crime had been discovered, all was forgiven. After her recovery from the acute stage of polio she tried to continue teaching but it proved impossible. Instead, thanks to the increasing popularity of the William stories, she could now devote all her time to writing, supporting herself and Clara and at the same time helping Gwen to establish a home for Tommy and me.

The very first published story, according to my mother in later years, was "Thomas", which had appeared in the *Girl's Own Paper* in 1918. It described a small boy's transformation from mother's darling, with curls and dressed in smocks, into a rougher real boy, the changeover being achieved by means of a fight with another boy – called William. However, Thomas is the main character and wins the fight, then commandeers his adversary's clothes. The rest of the story concerns his mother's unexpected acceptance of the new tough image. My mother always attributed this story to

51

Richmal's observation of Tommy's character at the Denmark Hill house.

Another of Richmal's stories published in 1918, "One Crowded Hour", featured a William-type boy called Robert Green, aged seven. In 1919, the hero of the story "Rice Mould" in *Home* magazine was finally given the name William and it was here that the character really began to develop. William stories were then published monthly in *Home* until the end of 1922, when another Newnes publication, *The Happy Mag*, took over and continued to publish the stories until a few months after the start of World War II. Two hardback books published by Newnes in 1922 – *Just-William* and *More William* – combined most of the stories that had appeared to date in these magazines. The stories were not intended for children – Richmal was writing *about* children *for* adults. By 1969 when she died there were 37 William books, the book of the 1939 William film, a play and an unfinished book which was eventually published in 1970. She also produced 40 adult novels and ten volumes of short stories. In an effort to make a change from William, Richmal had written two books of stories about a boy called Jimmy, but he was only a weak imitation.

Richmal was really much more interested in writing her novels of family dramas and her first, *The Innermost Room*, was published in 1923, followed by *The Hidden Light* in 1924, then *Anne Morrison* in 1925. Each of these books was to some extent autobiographical, which can be seen in the character of the heroine, her friends and relatives. Other books of similar type followed regularly in quick succession. She preferred her more serious books to William but her publisher insisted on a monthly William story and Richmal in any case needed the regular income.

She had started writing at a very early age when playing alone in the attic of her home, reading her stories and poems to a doll. Under her father's guidance she read a great deal of poetry so it was not surprising that her first efforts were rhyming verses. She and her younger brother Jack were set a programme of work even in the school holidays, to broaden their minds and make sure their knowledge was well advanced. Their father had stuck a map of Europe on the bathroom wall in order to illustrate geography lessons.

Richmal rarely went out to play with girls of her own age,

as Gwen did, although she attended a small private school nearby. She was regarded as delicate but her own shy retiring nature may have accounted for her reluctance to join in "rough" games. When Richmal was ten, Gwen went off to St Elphins boarding school for the daughters of clergymen, and a year later Richmal followed.

She obviously enjoyed St Elphins. For the first time in her life she was surrounded by intelligent girls eager to make progress. She was no longer regarded as "different" and made to rest, as at home. Those days were behind her and she could now enter into all the school's activities. She started to develop her talent for writing in her early teens with contributions to the school magazine. Later she kept a Private Eye type of journal containing satirical descriptions of school personalities and events, which she allowed selected friends to read. However, it was all very innocent. Girls at that time had no means of learning sexual facts and were taught to avoid any thoughts in that direction since it was "evil". The existence of homosexual tendencies was never acknowledged even though the younger girls often had "crushes" on older monitors or staff, as in most boarding schools – and day schools for that matter.

Regimentation and strict discipline were the order of the day. The school was run very much on the lines of Cheltenham Ladies' College, which I was to experience a quarter of a century later. The St Elphins headmistress, Miss Kennedy, had been a strong admirer of Cheltenham and its principal, Miss Beale. But after Miss Kennedy's unexpected death in 1910 she was succeeded by Margaret Flood, who was later to be my godmother, and to give me her name, although I cannot remember ever meeting her. She lived to be well over 90 and wrote to me occasionally towards the end of her life. One of the reasons for this neglect had been her refusal to speak to Richmal between 1925 and the 1950s – she claimed to have recognised herself and St Elphins in Richmal's novel *Anne Morrison*, depicted in a very unflattering way.

The standard of education at St Elphins was progressive, creating an environment in which the Lamburn sisters could flourish. Richmal had spent so much more time with her father, absorbing the groundwork of Latin and Greek and very early reading Homer's Iliad, that she outshone Gwen, who in turn was better at Maths and French and also had artistic and musical talents. St Elphins measured its educational success by the number of girls who obtained scholarships and university places. Social graces were not high on the list of required achievements but correct manners were – even to the wearing of gloves in the school grounds to

Richmal aged 13

(8)

in the dini

when I wen

gone but A

Antie Ada

"Ray we've bee

meeli

are l

— M

I wish you could

All him he's the darling-

-est fish that ever lived & so

good too, you must look

at him first thing you

come home. Mother had

a meeting of the refreshment

stall committee (Bazaar)

& they were a long time.

With love of loves

I Remaing

Your Ray loving sister

PS I have not exchanged my

Richmal aged 10 writes to Gwen at school

protect the girls' hands. Games gradually gained an important status and St Elphins students were encouraged to play hockey, cricket and tennis, which both Gwen and Richmal enjoyed.

Amateur dramatics were encouraged and secret societies flourished. Richmal ran a secret literary society in which each member produced a weekly contribution for comment by the others and votes were taken on the best. The small select society met rather openly in a hidden corner of the grounds, which were not really extensive enough to escape the notice of others. According to my mother, there were many cliques of girls getting together discreetly in gangs without any particular aims or functions. There were definitely no outlaws, however, owing to the harsh punishments handed out for the smallest of misdemeanours.

Just as Richmal was later to poke fun at authority through the William books, here at school she took the same line when writing school plays and humorous features. She was an early "mickey-taker" who dared to express it in writing. Gwen was a more solid and serious person and did not have the same sense of humour. There was a certain amount of wit and satire in Richmal's writing at that time, but it was not actually cruel. Eventually she developed several different styles of writing, specialising in the art of the short story. It is thought that she had to make several efforts to get her work published before anything was finally accepted, and that even now there are one or two stories published but not yet identified.

Being principally a clergy daughters' school, although beginning to accept non-clergy fee-paying students during Gwen's and Richmal's time, St Elphins naturally placed much emphasis on religious education. Visiting curates, who were occasionally young and handsome, caused a certain amount of excitement amongst the girls. But there was nothing to prepare Gwen for the type of man she was to marry, nor was there anyone like him in her home life, amongst friends and neighbours. Her education had encouraged her to assume that all men were honest, noble and chivalrous although not necessarily kind, and her own observation had taught her that some were very interesting but a great many were bores. Perhaps she should have taken a closer look at Dickens. Fortunately Edward and Clara

Lamburn had made an early decision that their daughters must acquire good qualifications so that they would be equipped for all life's eventualities. It was almost as if they had sensed that Gwen would have to fight to support her family and that Richmal would meet a physical calamity that would leave her dependent on her intellect.

By 1910 Gwen was studying at home for an external London University degree and Richmal had become a student teacher at St Elphins. In 1911, she won a scholarship to Royal Holloway College, part of London University, from where she graduated with a classics degree in 1914 and returned once again to St Elphins to teach. But she wanted to be near her mother and sister – brother Jack had already left for Africa in 1913 – and so in the autumn of 1917 she took up a teaching post at Bromley High School in Kent.

In my childhood Richmal was still seeing her old school friends and university colleagues either in London or at the Denmark Hill house, which provided a good meeting place. In the following years she kept up these friendships, adding those made at the High School in Bromley. She recounted all the news and gossip to my mother, who knew many of the same people. Once Richmal's own house, The Glebe, had been built in Bromley Common it became the new meeting place, especially valuable for visitors from the North. We were brought up to believe that Northerners, particularly Lancastrians, were the salt of the earth. A joking battle against Yorkshire was still kept up but although I knew we came from the right side of the Pennines, I could never remember whether I was a white or a red rose.

As she became famous, Richmal made new friends in many different walks of life and professions. She attended numerous functions in London including literary meetings and lunches; she never allowed her lame leg to restrict her social and professional life, although she found crowds a hazard. So – she remarked – she had to avoid the first day of the Sales! Not unnaturally she received a substantial fan mail from people all over the world and, being very susceptible to flattery, she used to joke about it, saying, "I love it – the more the better. They can never lay it on too thick." Acquaintances often fawned over her, which I found very irritating. After her death numerous people said, "Of course, Richmal and I were very close friends for many years," which made me laugh, because if they had really known her well they would have called her Ray, as all the family did.

Although people often assume that Richmal is a man's name, in our family it has always been given to girls. It was first recorded in the Bury area as early as 1705. My great-grandmother was Richmal Openshaw, who married a John Crompton so becoming the first Richmal Crompton. One of her five daughters was also called Richmal (Ellen) Crompton. She was my great-aunt, whom I met several times, so we were quite used to the name. But the woman the world knew as Richmal Crompton was in fact Richmal Crompton Lamburn.

Richmal Mangnall, the originator of Mangnall's *Questions*, was thought to be a distant relative. She was born in Manchester in 1769 and her *Questions*, mainly concerned with History and Antiquity, were privately published in 1800 and later acquired by the publishers Longman. For young ladies of the 19th century, the Questions and their Answers were next in importance to the Bible; girls were encouraged to use it as a manual for general education and to learn the contents by heart. It was in a way a substitute for education. But Richmal Mangnall, headmistress of Crofton Hall in Yorkshire for many years, also earned the undying gratitude of nearly every governess in the land, partly because the first edition was a small pocket volume, easily hidden under needlework.

Crompton has for centuries been a well known name in Lancashire but some scions must surely have emigrated to other counties. Colonel Crompton of the Crompton Parkinson electrical company, a Lancastrian with Yorkshire connections, wrote to Aunt Richmal after the publication of *Just-William*. She recognised the Lancastrian Crompton coat of arms in a stained-glass window in his London home when she went to see him. There was no evidence of a direct relationship, but the two became firm friends and she was fascinated by his tales of adventure. He was by then in his seventies, but in his youth had been an ADC attached to the Hapsburg court in Vienna, being one of the principal courtiers asked to break the news to the Empress Elizabeth of Prince Rudolph's suicide in 1889. I have often wondered why he was selected to console the Empress; but on seeing the ballet *Mayerling* I noted that a young British officer at the court was frequently at her side . . .

Colonel Crompton told Aunt Richmal that when his company had put electric light into Buckingham Palace, Queen Victoria had slapped his face. On her return from these visits Richmal would retell every detail, yet I cannot remember why his face was slapped. I doubt that Victoria was the face-slapping type – perhaps the lights had all fused at the switch-on or perhaps an old man had been romanticising.

Richmal continued to visit him throughout the 1920s and 1930s. She dedicated *Still William* published in 1925 to him: "Colonel R.F. Crompton, CB, RE". I never heard her use his first name. Then at the start of the war his two elderly daughters made him move to Ripon in Yorkshire, where he died soon afterwards in 1940, aged just over 90. Aunt Richmal always maintained that he died of cold in the old Yorkshire stone house in that very bitter winter of 1939/40. When his death was announced he was credited with the research and development that led to the invention of the tank, which made its first appearance in active service in 1916. His was the only dedication of a William book outside the immediate family until 1939, when Richmal chose the young actors who played the Outlaws in the William film for the dedication of *William and A.R.P.* They were Dick Lupino, Roddy McDowall, Peter Miles and Norman Robinson, who played William, Ginger, Henry and Douglas respectively.

As for the older generation of Crompton relatives, our great-grandfather John Battersby Crompton, Aunt Richmal's grandfather, killed himself by drinking prussic acid. As a chemist he must have known what he was doing and one might have expected a less painful method. That day, soon after he had gone to his chemist's storeroom, an apprentice found him dead with the bottle beside him. None of his family or friends admitted to knowing a reason but fortunately the coroner's court gave a verdict of temporary insanity. Photographs of him show the face of a kindly-looking handsome man, quite relaxed. His wife, my great-grandmother Richmal, looks tight-lipped, narrow-eyed and grim; although from all family accounts she was not unpopular with her children and grandchildren, despite her strict demeanour. She had borne eleven children, losing four of them either at birth or when very young.

The women of the Crompton family were stronger

characters than the men. The five daughters of John and Richmal Crompton dominated the household, putting the two sons Harry and Jack in the shade. Hannah and Lizzie were the two oldest, Clara was in the middle whilst Ada and Re (Richmal Ellen) were younger. We liked Ada best. I think she always admired Clara and one could tell they were close friends. She was, from the children's point of view, a "good sport" and had a sense of humour. Yet it was sad that her two sons – her only children – were both killed in the 1914-18 war. Lizzie and Re appeared as typical spinsters of the time, busily engaged in good works and dressed – at least, every time I saw them – in clothes of a bygone age.

The Crompton clan: our great-grandparents, great-uncles and great-aunts. Back row, extreme right: our very own Clara.

I do not remember Hannah at all; perhaps she never visited The Glebe, but her son John Wrigley moved to the London area and became a distinguished civil servant who was eventually knighted. Months before World War II he had planned the evacuation of children from London and other main cities, into the countryside. Aunt Richmal often took his children Christopher, Martin and Elizabeth to theatres in

London and she dedicated *William's Happy Days* to them in 1930. Clara's niece Rene – Harry Crompton's only daughter, also christened Richmal – was on good terms with the Lamburns and often stayed at The Glebe.

My two unmarried great-aunts, Lizzie and Re, grew old together in Bury and every now and then visited London and Bromley, staying first at Cherry Orchard Road and then at The Glebe. A charity house in Bury, now demolished, was called Richmal Crompton House after Aunt Re in recognition of her services to the local Charity Services Organization, the CSO. In old age she and Aunt Lizzie lived very frugally, preferring to wear many cardigans rather than light a fire, or so it was said. At some stage they had a radio "on the parish", the equivalent of the Social Services at that time. They came to London with an umbrella full of holes, with panels that had lost their moorings and retreated up the frame, which Tommy and I thought hilarious. When they went up to London for the day to visit the shops they took their pennyworth of bus fare as far as possible, then walked back to wherever they had really wanted to go. In the 1930s it cost only a penny from Victoria Station to Marble Arch, so they had a long walk back to Piccadilly, when that was their target; though at least they had a good view of the park. But perhaps we were unfair. Only in recent years have I wondered how John Crompton's widow and unmarried daughters financed themselves after his suicide.

Aunt Ada, Aunt Richmal's favourite, used to tease the children. She was perhaps the prototype of the more attractive aunt that William liked. At the age of ten Richmal wrote to Gwen at school: "Mother had a meeting of the refreshment stall committee (Bazaar) and they were a long time in the dining room and when I went in (all had gone but Auntie Ada) Auntie said 'Ray, we've been having a meeting and no children are to sell anything off the refreshment stall.' Oh! I did feel mad although I pretended I didn't care a pin. I'm sure I was nearly crying. All at once she burst out laughing and they had not said anything of the sort and she had said it to tease me. I told Mother when she came in and Auntie Ada said she told me because I looked so miserable. I thought I'd been looking as happy as happy." So apparently Ada could go too far.

Another "aunt" from Bury who came to stay was Clara's

lifelong friend Mary Roberts, who was also Gwen's godmother. She came to The Glebe for a week or two now and then. She was so normal that I remember almost nothing else about her. She was good for tips, though, as were the others. We could be fairly sure of five shillings each when any of them left for home. During the war I found myself unexpectedly near Bury and managed to find one of the family's addresses. I met Auntie Mary's relatives but was there for such a short time that they could not assemble the family or gather the clan.

On the other side of my mother's family, great-grandfather Edward Lamburn (father of Clara's husband, the Rev. Edward Lamburn) more or less drank himself to death. He had been a schoolmaster all his working life but having become an alcoholic at an early age he had to keep moving from school to school. He moved from the Aylesbury area to Derbyshire, then to several other parts of England including Liverpool, Macclesfield, Leeds and finally Wiltshire, where he died in 1898. His eldest son, Edward Lamburn junior (eventually father of Gwen, Richmal and Jack), became a schoolmaster-priest, teaching at Bury Grammar School and at the weekends taking church services in far-flung villages. He was a curate at Radcliffe Parish Church, very close to Bury, and took locum work in the school holidays; once he held a temporary chaplaincy at the lunatic asylum in Lancaster, where he put his family into lodgings nearby for a few weeks to give them a holiday. He had met Clara through teaching her younger brother Jack, the name they were later to give to their own son.

Edward did not at first sight fit into the preconceived idea of a popular schoolteacher. He was a very strict disciplinarian, yet his pupils tried endless small tricks to provoke and embarrass him. However, underneath the schoolboy banter was a deep respect for the Reverend's unselfish lifestyle and his saintly outlook on life and duty. He was affectionately known as "Lammy" and as he grew older he assumed a Mr. Chips role in the school.

Some time ago, while spending an hour or two waiting between trains at Crewe station, I found myself talking to another traveller, equally impatient of train delays. He turned out to be a native of Bury, and by then a director of Lewis's Ltd which at that time owned Selfridges and other stores, and when I mentioned that my grandfather had taught at Bury Grammar School, his whole face lighted up. "Lammy's granddaughter!" he said and stretched out his arms as if in welcome. "Lammy's granddaughter!" as if he could not believe it. He told me that my grandfather's pupils had had a very sincere affection for the man. The boys had not realised until after they left school how much they owed him for his insistence on high educational and moral standards. His guidance in defining the difference between right and wrong had served them well in any difficult situation they had encountered later in life.

There is no doubt that he had demanded from his own three children even higher standards. Their every action was liable to affectionate but firm correction. They were often hurt and disappointed by what seemed to be a lack of

"Lammy", Clara, Gwen, Jack and Ray (Richmal)

appreciation of their efforts. There is no evidence that he had a sense of humour like Richmal's, which would have helped the relationship with his children. Jack was the only other one who developed something of the same gentle mocking wit and sense of the ridiculous.

Profoundly depressed by his own father's drink problem, Edward took care that his children were constantly reminded of alcohol's dangers as a drug. In this respect he had identical views to those of Tom Disher senior. Aunt Re had made the Lamburn children join the Band of Hope and sign The Pledge but all three abandoned their promise long before they reached middle age, having found themselves rather partial to the demon drink.

Though not as ambitious intellectually as Hannah, the eldest of the Crompton brood, Clara was nevertheless highly intelligent and possessed a remarkable talent for organising. The young 32-year-old curate Edward Lamburn had proposed to Clara, then aged 24, by letter and she had accepted him in the same manner; all on a rather formal basis. By the time they were married on August 1st 1888 they had known each other for six years, having been engaged for two and a half years. Clara was the second of the five Crompton sisters to marry – three and a half years before their father killed himself.

By that time Clara and Edward had two children, Gwen having been born in June 1889 and Richmal in November 1890. Jack was not born until 1893, after the parental

Clara in her forties   The Lamburn children: Gwen, Jack and Ray

tragedy. There was to be another death, this time within the Lamburn family: Edward's and Clara's fourth child, Phyllis, died from whooping cough at the age of fourteen months in 1895. Jack was once again the "baby" of the Lamburn children. Although the depressing experience of Phyllis's early death drew the remaining three much closer, the five years separating Gwen and Jack naturally resulted in their having different interests. Richmal – in the middle – was close to both of them and in later years when all three were in their sixties and seventies, one of Richmal's principal aims was to help support her brother and sister.

Although Clara was kept very busy it was Edward who got up at 5.00 am, made the breakfast and stoked up the fire before going off for his early morning swim. In winter he often had to break the ice on the local reservoir, to take his swim before going on to a church service, which preceded his day's teaching at Bury Grammar School. He walked nearly everywhere, only occasionally using a bicycle. Clara had only a "daily" general maid to help with the cleaning and cooking, making jam, bottling fruit and preserving vegetables; she was also much occupied by her charitable and social duties as the wife of a curate and mother of three children. After leaving Bury she continued much of her work for charities: Waifs and Strays, Dr. Barnardos and Homes for Fallen Women stand out particularly in my mind. As a child I could not understand why fallen women did not get up again, or why they needed special homes. But I got evasive answers to my questions.

Looking again at the family photos, I remember my mother Gwen telling me that while Clara was expecting her she had prayed every night that if the child were a girl she would not be beautiful. In her view, beautiful women had great difficulty in achieving a good character. They were subjected to great temptations and their egos were inflated by frequent admiration, which resulted in vanity and selfishness. Her daily prayers were fairly successful with my mother. Presumably she said the same prayers for Richmal, again with moderately successful results. However, this second daughter had a delicate and interesting face. What of Clara herself? Of course I am biased, for I thought she was beautiful in old age. Looking at the five sisters in their young womanhood I think Clara stands out as handsome and attractive, the best of the group; but perhaps she was also a little spoiled by admiration.

As for the Reverend Edward, it is difficult to read anything into his expressionless face. He looks less like a waxwork in the rare photographs that reveal him without the droopy moustache but there is no doubt that he was a near-saint, determined to do his duty by God and his family. Clara held the purse strings, not trusting him to handle money. Once, having decided he needed a new overcoat, she gave him the cash to buy it on his way home from the Grammar School. He returned empty-handed and when pressed for an explanation said: "Well, I met Mrs Ramsbottom and you know her husband is still out of work – well, he's just got pneumonia. They've just had a new baby – that makes ten children now – so I really felt their need was greater than mine and gave her the money. I can manage quite a while longer with my old coat." This action was typical of the man, who lived a very unselfish life.

Edward had hoped his son would follow him into the Church but the idea did not appeal to Jack. His extremely strict upbringing had tended to spoil the relationship with his father, whereas Richmal had put Edward on a pedestal and from all accounts the high regard and affection she felt for him was justified. He was a most attentive husband to Clara, a responsible father and took all his duties to students and parishioners extremely seriously. His own lifestyle was very spartan and self-disciplined. I am sorry that I never met him – he died before I was born.

Jack had upset his father and disappointed the rest of the family by stopping his studies at Manchester University and joining the Rhodesian Mounted Police as a trooper. After a stiff recruits' course, he was posted to various remote up-country outstations in what is now Zimbabwe. At first he spent his spare time big-game shooting, but soon came to hate slaughtering such magnificent creatures. He continued, however, to stalk and lie in wait for them, but without a rifle. He came to have a great understanding and love for the big game, just as he had always loved the small animals and insects of the English countryside. But equally the insect life in Africa was conspicuous, to say the least, and Jack found the lives and customs of these small creatures more mysterious and complicated than the large ones, and never tired of watching them. So while his fellow troopers were complaining of boredom, Jack was fully entertained by an interest that was to become his future profession.

He left Africa in 1919 on completion of his contract and went to China to work for Butterfield and Swire, the British merchant company at that time dealing in shipping, insurance and sugar-refining. He remained in China for 12 years and during the first eight his job was to inspect the books and work of the Chinese agents. This meant travelling to remote towns by house-boat, Chinese junk, sampan, Peking cart, wheelbarrow and other unusual forms of transport. These journeys often took months. Few of the inhabitants of the interior towns had ever seen a white man before and the streets would be packed with people, as if for royalty. Crowds would follow behind Jack and his interpreter, all of them wanting to see what a "foreign devil" looked like, and his appearance usually caused shrieks of laughter. He even had to deal with bandits on the Yangtze River who were raiding the company's stores and sometimes kidnapping the employees. He wrote home frequently and Richmal was fascinated by this world so different from her own.

Jack Lamburn aged 18 (standing) and 20

Another Lamburn adventurer who could have inspired William's dreams was Richmal's cousin Robin Lamburn, who went out to Africa when just over 30 years old in 1935 and is still there. Both Robin and his brother Teddy, nephews of Edward Lamburn, entered the Church. Robin had studied pathology in addition to theology at Oxford, which proved to be an invaluable advantage for his later work in Tanzania – dedicated to the elimination of leprosy in the Rufiji river basin, 100 miles south of Dar-es-Salaam. The village where he is based has no electricity or running water; the only outside contact is through a battery-operated radio and an old semi-functioning telephone. During the rainy season the roads are impassable; the huge Rufiji river becomes a mass of brown swirling water, inhabited by hippos, which cause casualties amongst natives trying to cross by dug-out canoes. William, of course, would have manoeuvred his canoe and rescued the unlucky natives – in his imagination. He had frequently expressed his longing to be a native himself.

I have not seen Robin since 1960, although he was in London in 1986 to receive the Albert Schweitzer Prize for the Humanities. He is now in his 80s, which I find hard to imagine since my principal memory is of a young, rather handsome Boy Scout leader. Yet when my own wandering feet reached Dar-es-Salaam, quite close to Robin, I became exhausted by the heat and kept creeping back gratefully to my air-conditioned hotel, with lots of running water and mod-cons.

V

Cherry Orchard Days

William must have gone to church on 2600 Sunday mornings, sometimes with a beetle or white rat but usually with his parents. He enjoyed his contribution to the hymns and psalms, although the nearby members of the congregation did not. He also attended Sunday School in the afternoons, occasionally going instead to the Bible Class for Sons and Daughters of Gentlefolk, also the Band of Hope. The influence of Richmal's own upbringing in Bury is apparent in the Brown family's church-going tradition, mentioned in a number of the books. William managed to disrupt many of these solemn occasions.

For our part we often joined Aunt Richmal and Granny at church on Sundays. Holy Trinity, the local Parish Church at Bromley Common, is quite picturesque, set amongst a group of old yew trees, standing at the junction of the main Hastings Road where Oakley Road forks off to Westerham. We managed to avoid Sunday School, held in the little hall behind the church, because we thought Mother could teach us about Lot's Wife and explain the other curious passages in the Bible.

The William stories making up the first nine books were written in the house at 9 Cherry Orchard Road, not far from the church. It was a friendly little road lined with lime trees, which had been there for at least 60 years. Then, just after World War I, the road consisted of several small Victorian houses opposite a Baptist chapel and a village shop selling groceries and domestic oddments. No.9 is a detached house with four up and two down, and a reasonably sized kitchen. The small size of the garden was quite a shock for us, coming from the larger grounds of the Denmark Hill house. Originally No.9 was only intended for Aunt Richmal and grandmother Clara but our mother lived with them while we were at the small Kent boarding school.

The two sisters, Richmal and our mother Gwen, had always been close and owing to Tom Disher's frequent absences abroad they were now together again. At first after leaving Denmark Hill we had taken rooms in Bromley, which

Photo: Doreen Spooner

William's birthplace: 9 Cherry Orchard Road, where the first nine books were written

Clara in middle age

were hateful, so we spent most of our time at Bromley Common, only a short bus ride away. Granny Clara was particularly pleased to see us when she was on her own during the term time, while Richmal was out all day teaching.

These were the days before Aunt Richmal caught polio and because we were for the most part fatherless she spent many hours playing with us, taking a very active part in our country expeditions. From Bromley Common we could reach Hayes Common, Keston Common and many attractive villages, most of them on the bus routes. After a year or two, Tommy found friends of his own age and so became less willing to come on family trips.

Tommy the climber

The pond at the end of Cherry Orchard Road

Bromley Common had everything a village needs: several large farms, extensive orchards, a village school and church hall behind Holy Trinity, an old rambling vicarage, a market garden, a policeman and a row of small shops on the Hastings Road – a butcher, baker, draper, wine merchant and post office. A large part of the local orchards was devoted to cherry trees, which suited us down to the ground. In adult years Tommy saw nothing strange in playing golf with a man whose cherry trees he had once stripped, but I found the situation distinctly odd.

At one end of Cherry Orchard Road, a short distance from No.9, was a beautiful pond with trees round the edge. Twenty years later the pond was drained and filled in with grass lawn, but in our day that was where Tommy found most of his interesting water creatures and where, aged only four, he had caught a "wild" duck. An old coaching inn on the main road – The Plough – was close to the pond, where years before there had also been a smithy's forge.

In our time old Mrs Harris of Oakley Farm, almost opposite the church, was very deaf and we had to shout into her ear trumpet. Her daughter Norah ran the farm. The attractive old farmhouse still stands in its rural setting amid woods and fields, spoiled only by the traffic roaring past and a large bus garage on the opposite side of the road. Several generations of the Harris family had run the farm by the time we came to live in the neighbourhood.

Across the main road opposite The Plough there used to be a large market garden, spread over several acres, with a wonderful assortment of potting sheds, outhouses, greenhouses and the central farmhouse. For me, this was the most exciting part of the village after the woods and the pond. The daughter of the Cooling family, who ran the place, was about my own age so I used to go there when Tommy went off with his Red Indian and pirate friends. Now it has all gone and in place of the potting sheds are small modern houses and a row of shops. After The Plough the main road going south rises up over Knowles hill towards Locksbottom and Farnborough. At that time the whole area consisted of fields and woods, which included Nobody's Wood. It is there today, presumably still unclaimed.

The second part of the village, where Richmal eventually lived, was half way along Oakley Road, which leads away

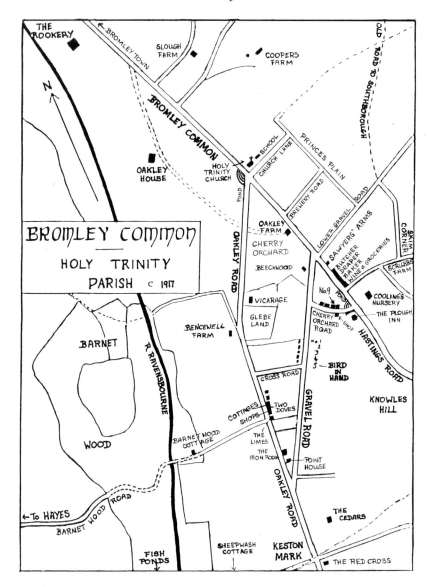

from the church towards Westerham. There was an easy short cut from the end of Cherry Orchard Road to this enclave of houses and shops. In 1927 Aunt Richmal was to build an attractive house there. This new house – The Glebe – was close to Barnet Wood Road, which bends and twists on its way to Hayes Common. Today there are livery stables opposite The Glebe, selling manure at 50p a bag, and I keep thinking what a fortune William could have made with this line of business. It could have solved his recurring financial problems.

Years later Oakley Road was to become well known to the RAF during the war as they drove at high speed to and from Biggin Hill airfield; the Battle of Britain was partly fought over Bromley Common and Hayes. We waved to our planes as they returned to base, often receiving a dipped-wing salute in return. I heard a story of a damaged Messerschmitt which calmly taxied along Oakley Road, waiting to be stopped and captured; but everyone was too astonished to do anything but stand and stare, thinking it was some kind of joke. I suppose eventually Captain Mainwaring and his Dad's Army arrested it for contravening traffic regulations!

Oakley Road led directly to Keston Common and its surrounding park. Although I loved Keston Woods, which were not far by bus, the Fish Ponds had a morbid reputation

Keston Fish Ponds: fascinating yet sinister

– I knew that several people had been drowned there. Huge water lilies grew over a large part of the water and although there were faded notices "Danger – Swimming Prohibited" we knew that from time to time people ignored the warnings and dived in, only to disappear for ever. They became trapped in the strong water-lily roots and were unable to reach the surface again. Even where the lilies were not visible the roots were there, ready to trap them. The ponds were said to be quite deep. I used to wonder how many bodies were in those murky depths, still wrapped in water lily roots.

Tommy was not bothered by such thoughts. He was intent on catching frogs. At the right stage of the season he would search for frog-spawn, then tadpoles, putting them into a water jar with some weeds, taking them home and studying every stage of their growth. I kept a safe distance but had to admit that the small frogs were rather sweet. At this stage we would tip them into the local Cherry Orchard pond and hope they would multiply. Newts were another favourite; Tommy loved them the way other people love dogs.

The Norman family owned The Rookery, a Queen Anne style country house, with lands adjoining Bromley Common. Unfortunately it was burned down in 1946 and the remainder demolished. In the third story in *Just-William* there is a similar house, possibly based on The Rookery, where William accidentally takes on the job of Boots boy – he would have had a small bedroom there if he had managed to keep the job for more than an hour. In our childhood most of the charity Sales of Work and garden fetes were held in The Rookery grounds, so Aunt Richmal and our grandmother knew the Normans, which made it seem less like trespassing when we wandered through their woods and fields. But sometimes we could hear gunshots not too far away, which made us realise it was dangerous – and we would probably get into trouble if we got shot and killed.

Tommy, an adventurous explorer one minute, would turn into a boy hero the next, escaping from gangs of criminals. He ran in and out of trees and thick bushes, looking continually behind him, prepared to climb trees for refuge if necessary and only stopping when he reached the safety of Barnet Wood Road, panting for breath. This was a rather lonely road with dense woods on either side, once past the few houses. There were sharp bends in the road and anything could be lying in wait beyond the next curve. No one would hear the explorer shout for help, but at least civilisation was within reach.

On a sunny summer day he would turn his attention to the small stream which ran through the woods, the start of the little River Ravensbourne. He imagined that the stream would deliver huge salmon and other rare fish if only he knew how to catch them. It had been easy in Tahiti because their bright colours could be seen so clearly. Here, when he found exciting-looking objects, they often turned out to be old boots thrown in by some tramp.

To Tommy, the tramps spelled glorious freedom from rules and regulations. But I was afraid of them. One pursued us steadily through a wood, gradually gaining ground. I sensed the evil intent, with mounting fear. Tommy was quite unaware of danger, for tramps were his friends. "Tommy, run – please!" I said, pushing ahead all the time towards where I knew the road would be. I wanted to run but hated to leave him behind. Fortunately he caught my sense of urgency and followed. We were able to outpace the lumbering tramp, but I have dreamed of that episode for years, because it was then that I first realised Tommy had no "receiving set" to alert him to potential danger.

In the William books the Outlaws' lifestyle is very familiar to me, for we knew the importance of a really good bow and well made arrows, backed up by a catapult (which was, of course, more easily replaced when lost). Pea-shooters were more difficult to aim except at a short distance and could not bring down a juicy apple. Pistols with caps were of little use except to frighten unsuspecting people. I never attempted tree-climbing but Tommy and his friends were just like monkeys. I hated their bird-nesting expeditions but at least they kept to the rules: never more than one egg per nest and never remove the whole nest unless the fledglings have gone. They knew every bird by the shell markings, whereas the eggs all looked the same to me. There was a system for removing the yolk, in order to preserve the shell, but I cannot remember how it was done.

Fights were frequent. Usually they were a cross between boxing and wrestling and included ear-pulling, hair-pulling and a good deal of kicking. The aim was to get the opponent on the ground and sit on him. When the boys were older all

this was legalised under the name "rugger". Tommy learned boxing and rugger from the age of nine but every now and again in adult years he forgot the strategic methods of self-preservation and suffered a fair number of injuries. He was also inclined to hit out when provoked.

All his life Tommy would tramp through the house in muddy boots, in later years after gardening, leaving his mother in despair, trying to clean up patches of mud everywhere. When he was young, dirty puddles and all ditches acted like a magnet, luring him to test the waterproofing of his boots and shoes. Wellingtons did not feature much in our lives; perhaps the children's variety of that time were damaged too easily, failing to withstand sharp stones and barbed wire. They were called "gumboots".

Stone-throwing was an important art. A boy's prestige with his peers was judged partly on his ability to throw a reasonably large stone not only a long way but also shorter distances very accurately and with considerable force. When the boys are grown up, that is called "bowling". But the height of artistry is to hit a moving object, such as a cat. It was all fair game and not at that time thought cruel; the cat generally escaped anyway, having a greater degree of agility than the small boys. Throwing small, short tree branches was another pastime, often performed to please a dog.

But ponds and streams were always the most fascinating part of the countryside. The longing to dangle one's feet in water is overwhelming. Sometimes feet get into the water accidentally; it is difficult to remember that stones and boulders are slippery with invisible slime, so that crossing even an easy-looking narrow part is not without difficulties. Jumping from one side to the other can also be hazardous; sometimes what looks like firm ground the other side turns out to be a squelchy bog. A boy who can jump streams without falling in needs to be agile. Tommy usually fell in.

Some of William's activities in the early books seem more appropriate for a younger boy. Possibly Aunt Richmal had difficulty in deciding his age at the start. It was not until the eleventh William story, published in *Home* magazine in 1920, that his age of eleven years was mentioned. The drawings are of a younger boy, who becomes taller as the first dozen books

progress. In some stories William and the Outlaws play with marbles and tops, which Tommy had finished with well before the age of eleven. This confirms that Richmal was watching a boy younger than eleven which confused her ideas of the age-group. (Her statement in one story is amusing by today's standards: "The Outlaws were topless", which conjures up a rather chilly image until the real meaning becomes clear – that they could not afford to buy spinning tops.) Conker-bashing, however, was taken very seriously well past eleven.

I still remember the terrible noise Tommy and his friends used to make with mouth organs, all playing different tunes at the same time. They kept the most extraordinary assortment of objects in their pockets and it could be seen that their handkerchiefs served many different purposes before they were "lost". About the age of eleven Tommy started to collect stamps and tried to contribute to Aunt Richmal's education by explaining the vital points of interest. In any case she looked to us for her information on the most popular sweets, cakes and fizzy drinks.

As for William's village, many readers have tried to track down its location. Aunt Richmal said it was an imaginary place and admitted that she set the houses here and there without any plan, accidentally changing them round from time to time. Yet it is remarkably similar to Bromley Common. William's village is within easy commuter distance of London and obviously well served by trains because Mr Brown goes up to the City every day; yet at the same time he is frequently around the house or visiting the neighbours, even on weekdays. Perhaps he only works from 11.00 till 3.00 pm! In the books the trains stop at the village and people walk from the station whereas the station for Bromley Common has always been Bromley South, nearly four miles away.

There are indeed many inconsistencies in Richmal's description of William's village, just as there are in the families and their names, which have been pointed out by William fans over the years. For example, William's favourite girlfriend – Joan – sometimes lives next door and at other times at the other end of the village, whichever suits the plot. Sometimes her name is Joan Clive and at other times Joan Crewe. The surnames of the Outlaws also vary occasionally from book to book.

I have looked at the Lamburns' old house in Bury's Chesham Road, where Richmal lived from the age of six to 25 – except in term times. I have wondered whether she retained that scene in her mind as a background for William; but although the house looks out over an expanse of green fields, with trees in the distance, the area was certainly not a village. It was within the boundaries of a sooty industrial town peppered with textile and paper mills, and is only now reverting to the more residential character it must have had before the mills arrived – before Aunt Richmal's time. In some of the stories there are hills and a small valley just outside William's village; these could have been taken from Bury, where the foothills of the Pennines start. But the character of Richmal's fictional village is much nearer to that of Bromley Common, where time stood still from the mid 19th century until World War I and then again until the late 1920s, when suburbia began to spread in that direction.

There was a Beechwood House in William's village; there was a Beechwood House at the end of Cherry Orchard Road. Other houses and cottages in the immediate Cherry Orchard vicinity were Hawthorn Cottage, Rose Cottage, The Limes and the big house The Cedars; all to be found in the William stories. I think Richmal avoided the more distinctive Bromley Common names such as Point House, Plough Cottages and Sheep Wash Cottage. It is difficult to find the name of the Browns' house in the books; they moved house at least once – which provided furniture-removing incidents for William. Eventually one finds the name The Hollies, but no doubt the name is not consistent.

All types of people lived at Bromley Common and they all knew each other and each other's mothers and fathers, sons and daughters. Local businesses, such as the building firm William Smith, who were also undertakers, were handed down from father to son. Retired professional people and the less wealthy relatives of landowners lived in the larger houses. An elderly Miss Holland of the gin family occupied a small estate not far from The Glebe.

Richmal once told me that she had to keep William's village rather vague in case people started jumping to conclusions and identifying themselves, with the inevitable result of hurt feelings and anger. She had already experienced this problem with some of her novels.

William's brother Robert and sister Ethel, Jumble the dog and the Outlaws – Ginger, Douglas and Henry – were all imaginary characters from the start of the stories. Tommy was a natural leader and always attracted a gang around him but his ginger-haired friend Peter Freeman did not turn up until 1924, at much the same time as Frank Masters. These two were his principal comrades and partners in crime from the age of nine onwards. It was coincidence that Peter's hair was ginger but everyone assumed he was the prototype for the

Outlaw. What I remember most clearly was his appetite for cake and the occasion when Aunt Richmal offered him the cake plate and he took the main part instead of the slice. There was a horrified silence and then Tommy exploded with fury.

"Jumble" had no opposite number in our family. It was many years before we had a dog and then – sadly – not for long. The Bury household of the Lamburn family was not known to keep dogs either. Clara had an obsessive loathing of cats all her life, so it is unlikely that any four-legged creature would have been welcome. The description of William's first meeting with Jumble indicates that Richmal understood the relationship between dog and man, and yet she never chose a dog for herself. However, a Pekinese named Ming was given to her in the late 1940s by her sister-in-law, Joan Lamburn, who was finding the dog a nuisance, and from then on Richmal became Ming's willing slave.

The Lamburn-Disher passion for insects runs through all the William books, mainly centred on William's attempts to "tame" them, attributing every movement – hop, jump or slither – to his own training of the creature. Both Tommy and

Jack adored them yet there is no way that Jack could have influenced Tommy; because Jack was in Africa until 1919, then China until 1930. It must have been coincidence, or some characteristic inherited from the Lamburns or Cromptons. Our mother Gwen screamed loudly the moment she saw a moth, so the insect-loving gene must have been rejected in her case – and mine. The Rev. Edward was not known to like insects; yet this peculiar trait was shared by both boys and there is hardly a pre-war William story that fails to feature crawly insects such as beetles, snails, slugs, worms, centipedes and earwigs or water creatures like tadpoles, frogs and newts – all of which compete with rats and mice for William's favour. Although Jack liked snakes, Tommy had no real acquaintance with reptiles. Both boys loved the large wild animals, though Jack was the only one who met them face-to-face.

VI

William Origins

One of the reasons for Tommy's dislike of being labelled the original William – and possibly this applied to Jack as well – was that the plots frequently involved the theft of the family's possessions and of food from larders, dining rooms, and other people's houses. Why do we laugh at this? Probably we would all have enjoyed indulging in open theft but were never allowed to do so. No-one lectures William about stealing so he often gets away with it. The most extreme case was the complete ransacking, not by William alone, of Mr. Moss's sweet shop in "William's New Year Day", during the owner's absence. But William is lucky, because Mr. Moss is so thrilled that his marriage proposal to his beloved has been accepted that he does not mind.

There is an important argument in William's defence – that food within his own home should be considered a communal possession and therefore it was not really stealing. The plot of "Rice Mould", the first William story published, rests solely on his efforts, eventually successful, to remove cream blancmange from his household's larder in order to please a small girl living next door, only to find he has mistakenly brought her the pudding she dislikes most in the world – rice mould. There is nothing else to the plot beyond the difficulties in achieving such a non-event, complicated by the presence of a cat which also gets into the larder.

We do not know the origins of this story but Tommy, with his own particular brand of logic, in this situation would have persuaded himself that chivalry was noble, excusing everything, justifying the removal of blancmange from the larder. Another argument – as he was not being allowed to attend the party that evening in his own family's house – could be that the blancmange was rightfully his share of the goodies. When very young, Tommy may indeed have taken cakes and puddings from the larder. After all, his father was in wholesale confectionery, so the opportunities were there despite shortages after the war. Like so many boys and men, Tommy loved food all his life. And all his life, like William, he cracked nuts almost continuously – finances permitting –

and left a trail of shells on the carpet.

Other things were stolen by the Outlaws that no tortured philosophy could justify. As for Tommy, I am not sure at what age his honesty matured, for it is probably a primeval instinct in a small boy to take what he wants until through punishment and instruction he stops. Tommy in his teens and when grown up was exceedingly honest but I cannot provide evidence about his childhood because his behaviour seemed quite normal to me: it was the grown-ups who were so peculiar. Even William has fits of blatant honesty, although generally he manages to convince himself he has the right to the object he has purloined or that he only intends to "borrow" it. Richmal's brother Jack would have found outright stealing impossible because of his father's strict discipline.

Tommy's honesty was reflected in "William's Truthful Christmas". Tommy was liable to upset the family's friends and neighbours by giving his truthful views when asked. When older he expressed strong views – unasked – about make-up (mostly mine), smoking, all the latest fashions for female hats, clothes and hair styles. Although a revolutionary he was also very conservative. We gave him presents with much trepidation because he never hesitated to reject anything that failed to please him. "Well, I'm sorry but it's a pity you didn't ask me before you bought that. Can't you take it back?" was often our reward for hours of patient searching through the shops. In the end there were only two safe things to choose. One was chocolate and the other was golf balls, although I was lucky once or twice with ties.

In "William's Truthful Christmas" he decides to spend the whole festive day being truthful. He has, for once, listened to the vicar's sermon and been inspired to cast aside deceit and hypocrisy. He gives very truthful answers when relatives ask whether he likes the presents they have given him. As a result he is accused of being ungrateful and Robert, for one, thinks he should be hanged. After upsetting family friends as well, with frank views on their appearance, William decides that holiness is not for him.

Tommy had the ability to convince himself that his fantasies were real. For example he was overheard describing his adventures swimming in Tahiti's lagoon, saying that he had been riding a shark. When reproached by his father he replied "Well, I swam in the lagoon and there were sharks there. How do you know that I did not ride one?" That was pure William.

Small boys are often boastful, mostly for the benefit of their own egos. William went to the extreme in "William and the Fairy Daffodil", telling a small girl he wished to impress that he had had all his teeth out – without gas. Then he went one further, saying his leg had been cut off, again without gas. This was an excessive economy with the truth but even so the little girl remained unimpressed. Frequently he claimed to be a famous explorer, a much feared pirate, a Red Indian chief; and all the Outlaws play-acted their fantasies, even to the point of becoming cannibals and eating each other. At some stage the dividing line between the imagination and the truth becomes blurred. At my own school, a very English-looking girl claimed to be a Chinese princess and wept buckets over the years because we refused to believe her.

Some of the William plots are, of course, exaggerated or at the very least embroidered. This is an essential element of the humour. William himself is a mixed-up eccentric character with a strong desire to help his friends, which include small girls and tramps – even at times his relatives – yet at the same time he has a very well developed desire for revenge when the occasion arises. He is incredibly obtuse, unable to see that a tramp has stolen the family silver even when it is falling out of his pockets; yet he is a very good and subtle strategist, with good planning ability. He has flashes of brilliance when at the eleventh hour he redeems an apparently hopeless situation. This again is a description of Tommy, who was very good at chess and bridge even at William's age, yet was completely defeated by bookwork and school learning.

The fight against boredom is the root cause of all William's adventures. His own village is too small for his vision of life, which leaves him a choice of searching out and creating his own adventures or living in a fantasy world. He does both. Meanwhile Tommy, having the same hunger for adventure, was more fortunate. He was provided with real-life adventures, mainly by his father who suffered from the same tendency, and partly through the adventure stories of his relatives – Uncle Jack and then Cousin Robin in Africa, and Uncle Maurice Disher who had contacts with stage stars, magicians, clowns and circus animals. What our parents noticed, and reported back to Aunt Richmal, was that while Tommy was experiencing real-life adventure in Tahiti and the USA, he was *not* engaged in his usual disruptive enterprises. One could say that he had reached his target. Once back in England, however, he must again create his own entertainment. He was not as imaginative as William, however, so his adventures were less bizarre.

Some of the stories are very complicated and quite a number have more than one plot. The third to be published (the first in the hardback *Just-William*), entitled "William goes to The Pictures", leads him into four different complications in the one story. This was pure flights of fancy based on William's efforts to emulate the entire film programme of several "shorts". Yet right at the end of nearly impossible situations Richmal uses her childhood memory of Jack experimenting with the paint on his bedroom door, discovering with triumph that the flame from a lighted taper will soften the paint so that it can be entirely removed, even from a large door panel, with a penknife blade.

My own appearance as a baby in the second published story "The Outlaws" provided a rather more substantial plot than "Rice Mould". Here William has been made to take a baby out in its pram for the afternoon. His shame at the thought of facing Ginger, Douglas and Henry makes William pretend he has kidnapped the baby and intends to demand a ransom. The baby is duly parked in the old barn, gets covered

in cooking oil, chews its bonnet strings and when confronted with a cow that Ginger has "found", welcomes it enthusiastically as a "bow-wow".

The real-life episode took place a few months before the first William story was written, when we were at the Harris's farm at Bromley Common. I was just beginning to talk and Tommy, having given up his attempts to lose me in the park at Denmark Hill, was now trying to take a hand in my education. He tried to make me relate each animal to its name and its noise but I gave the wrong answer every time, saying "bow-wow" when confronted with a cow, a goat, a pig and chickens and making the identical fierce growl for each of them. Undaunted by such stupidity, Tommy continued his encouragement, saying "That's right, Baby" whatever I said, which became a family catch-phrase for the rest of our lives and the story was retold by my mother many times. In the William story, the Outlaws find a ransom difficult to demand, so they return the baby to its owner, a friend of William's mother, in a very grubby condition. Even the pram has passed through a few adventures.

Richmal's own teaching observations provide the theme for the fourth story in *Just-William*, "The Fall of the Idol", in which a scholastically obtuse William becomes enamoured with a young and pretty teacher who tries – without success – to make him understand compound interest. He denudes his family's conservatory of all its flowers in order to provide a suitable offering; he actually does his homework whilst at the same time planning to marry the teacher, but gets into so many complications when trying to please her that he eventually gives up and goes back to his old bachelor life.

In later books William is depicted as a girl-despiser, a true misogynist; but in virtually every story of the early books there is a small girl that he generally tries to please or impress. William also blushes frequently. The little girls are always pretty and attractively dressed. Even a London East End visitor to the countryside has her own attractive style. When William selects prospective partners for dancing – his own style of dancing – he makes a rapid assessment of the girls' attractions one by one but in each case allows someone else to get there first. He is not attracted by the butch type of girl – he likes them pretty and feminine and with capabilities inferior to his own, so that they will admire him. Richmal frequently draws attention to their auburn curls and blue eyes. Even Ethel, William's older sister, has auburn hair and blue eyes; however, William then considers her plain and elderly, failing to understand why she is attractive to others. Violet Elizabeth does not appear until May 1924, in the 56th story "The Sweet Little Girl in White", which also appeared in the *Still William* hardback of 1925. But there were many girls in William's life before her and although she adores him, he spurns her attentions whenever possible.

"William Joins the Band of Hope", another story in *Just-William*, is based on Richmal's own childhood. Her Aunt Re actually ran the local Band of Hope in the Bury area. She was a great social worker in the broadest sense and Richmal soon saw the comic side of self-righteous workers for the good of mankind. Tommy's influence comes into the same story, when William tranforms a sedate children's group at a Band of Hope meeting into a scene of tigers and trainers. Tommy's realistic wild-animal imitations had caused consternation and alarm amongst little girls from quite an early age.

In "William's Secret Society" there are echoes of the Reverend Edward's methods of disciplining boys who absconded from their lessons. In this story, after William has left his classroom via a window, the schoolmaster follows him home, to intercept his escape. This is almost exactly what Edward Lamburn once did when one of his Bury Grammar School students thought he could avoid a detention. But William wants revenge on his tormentor, so joins forces with three boys (not the Outlaws) who on his behalf wreak vengeance on the schoolmaster in many small ways – wasps in his boots, deflated bicycle tyres, soot in his hat and so on.

Other stories are derived from Aunt Richmal's own experiences and observations as a child and schoolgirl. My mother recognised in the William books the Very Important Visitors who came to their own boarding school St Elphins, either to give a lecture or to present prizes. And amateur dramatics, which flourished in the Crompton family and probably nearly every other family of that time, were also popular with the girls of St Elphins: they used to write their own plays and act in them. The same type of entertainment takes place in William's village in nearly every book, and the amateur style of the production is always good for a send-up.

In Richmal's schooldays "plays" were encouraged from tots to teen alike and acted with the help of massive prompting. It is a theme that recurs throughout the books; in fact there are sometimes two amateur theatricals in one book, which provides scope for endless charades. In "What Delayed the Great Man", the play is written and acted by William; whereas in another story he is responsible only for noises off-stage, ranging from high winds, rain and thunder to horses' hooves, which he carries out with such exuberance and to such comic effect that a famous actor in the audience sends him tickets for the first night of his own next show in London. Tommy had a definite gift for simulating every known noise (largely intended to frighten people he did not like), so Richmal could always tune in to a good selection for special effects in her stories. Acting and the theatre were always important in her own life.

Richmal's own memories are again apparent in *William in Trouble* (dedicated to me aged 9). She had organised a secret literary society when a schoolgirl at St Elphins; the members voted each week on the others' creative efforts and the winner was given a badge. In "William among the Poets" the elder brothers of two of the Outlaws and several of their friends form a secret society of poets – secret mainly to avoid the Outlaws. They meet once a week and award a badge to the winner. When they decide to enter a competition being held by the local newspaper, the plot becomes, as usual, rather complex and includes a variety of misunderstandings.

In several William stories the Outlaws mislead some unsuspecting visitor to the village, taking him on a route march all round the neighbouring fields, even up a hill, in order to prevent visits to their homes or to kidnap the person for some complicated motive instead of guiding him to where he wanted to go. Invariably they get the wrong man, or the right man for the wrong reason. This happens in "William among the Poets", which is based on Tommy's deliberate misdirection of a family friend to Aunt Richmal's house because he thought the man was a farmer's lawyer about to lodge a complaint with my mother. He did not think far enough ahead to realise that the man would find the correct direction in the end and would not for long be put off by a small boy.

Hockey, one of Richmal's favourite sports before she

caught polio, features in the story "The Magic Monkey". Even in her late twenties she played for the staff team in matches against the girls of Bromley High School. In this story the Outlaws use their fathers' walking sticks to play hockey – according to their own rules. They have watched what seems to them an extraordinary game being played by girls at a local school; but after learning that men also play hockey, they enter into the sport with considerable enthusiasm and not a little damage to themselves and the walking sticks.

Although Richmal must have been to the circus as a child, she was still very much interested in Uncle Maurice's stories which Tommy and I used to recount. In my early teens he took me to Sanger's famous circus and we went to Dame Laura Knight's caravan where she was painting the animals and circus scenes. He was regarded as *the* expert on the subject and his books included "Clown" and "The Greatest Show on Earth". In the fifteenth William story "The Circus", William and his grandfather (there is sparse mention of grandparents, although William has an endless supply of aunts and great-aunts) escape secretly from the Brown's

house in the late evening after both have been sent to bed early, for different reasons, and manage to reach the local circus. Richmal's vivid description is certainly enough to rekindle any reader's interest in the clowns, acrobats, fierce performing animals, horses, ringmaster and the girl rider in frilly skirts. A sub-plot at the start of the same story gives a description of William at his dancing class. This was exactly Tommy, who was unable to follow the teacher's instructions, was to slow to keep up with the music and upset the little girls by treading on their toes. Although at that time he was only five years old he soon reached a stage when they all refused to dance with him.

Two of Tommy's insect calamities appear in the second hardback book *More William*, although attributed to a smaller boy. In "A Busy Day", when three aunts are staying in the Brown household, a small cousin's tin of snails gets accidentally left open and they escape, leaving a trail of slime on clothes, umbrellas and wallpaper, which William helps to clean up early one morning before the adults find out. In the cleaning process, which ends in a water battle between William and his cousin, everything within sight becomes soaked. Yet there is no sign of the snails. There are several plots within the one story, mainly concerning unsuccessful mechanical experiments by William, first with a clock and secondly with a kitchen mincing-machine. Both experiments end in disaster although he claims to have followed instructions in a book *Things a Boy Can Do*; the end result is a medley of nuts, bolts, springs and cog-wheels on the floor. I made a brief appearance in this story as a diminuitive female cousin who settles down to breakfast asking proudly, "Did you hear me clean my teef?"

The tin of snails was a real-life episode at our house in Denmark Hill although that did not end in the watery mess that William managed to produce. Some of the snails were recaptured but others disappeared forever. The damage to clothes was an entirely separate incident, made by slugs Tommy kept in his coat pocket. There was a great fuss about this episode, at the small hotel where we were having a holiday in Falmouth, with Tommy upset about the loss of his slugs while the guests were left to clean up their own possessions, with many apologies from our mother. The general attitude of the hotel guests was resentful, to say the least, whenever they set eyes on Tommy, as described in the story "William and the Smugglers".

Tommy's collection of wasps in a paper bag was immortalised in *More William* in a plot where another small boy (called Thomas) keeps snails in his pocket, woodlice and worms in another, and "wopses" in a paper bag. This is exactly what Tommy called his live wasp collection and his efforts to collect them resulted in so many stings that his face swelled up, to leave only slits for his eyes and his fingers ballooned to nearly double their normal size, leaving no gaps. In this story the small boy pressurises William into collecting more wasps, which sting him, then into scooping up more tadpoles and other swimming objects in a neighbouring pond. William is finally commanded to pick blackberries for the small boy to eat. William complies with all these autocratic demands, only to be fiercely reprimanded by the boy's mother, who suddenly appears on the scene and accuses William of leading her son into mischief. In this story, it is the small boy rather than William who is based on Tommy. William, for once, is the fall guy.

In the story "William's Hobby" it is definitely Tommy's dead frog which William thinks is being resuscitated in a cup of tea. In real life, the contents of the teacup were not being drunk by a visitor but merely discovered by our mother.

Six-year-old Tommy had heard grown-ups say that a nice cup of tea revived them even when they were absolutely dead, which led to his hopeful but unsuccessful treatment of the dead frog he had found.

When we read Sexton Blake detective stories, William read Sexton Blake. When we wrought havoc with miniscule balls of sealing wax, William did the same. After we climbed over planks of wood, bricks, scaffolding and got stuck in cement in a building site, William did the same – accompanied by his adopted "orphan", who fell into the cement. Unfortunately he was wearing William's best suit, presumably with the matching waistcoat shown in so many of Thomas Henry's drawings.

The pond at the end of Cherry Orchard Road had a highly climbable tree leaning well over the water. Tommy's foot slipped more than once, but the pond was not deep. In *William the Bad* William climbs a tree which leans over a pond and, of course, falls into the water. There was a water tunnel under Barnet Wood Road, crossing from one part of the wood to the other, allowing the little River Ravensbourne to pass through unmolested except by small boys who liked to try crawling through. William's clothes suffered once more when he tried a similar experiment in one of the stories. It was all there at Bromley Common except for a real river. Near William's village, people had picnics on the banks of a river – never possible, however, with the Ravensbourne, which on leaving Keston and the Rookery estate meandered alongside some allotments near Bromley South railway line before disappearing in its search for the Thames.

In "The May King", Tommy's peaked cap appears. Normally he hated caps or hats because they were compulsory for all schoolboys; but a train driver's cap was another matter and could be accompanied by much hooting, puffing and whistling. In the William story he uses the peaked cap to crown himself May King, standing beside his May Queen, the latest little girl to have won his affections. He has outwitted the originally selected May Queen by providing a tempting selection of cream cakes and jellies, spread out for her in a shed some distance away, and in her place he has manoeuvred another small girl; his own choice for May Queen. In real life Tommy claimed to be King of the Greens – all shades of green were his property and he wore his green

peaked cap to prove it. He lost it in 1921 at the small children's boarding school in Kent and we never found who stole it. One of the photos taken there shows him in a clean new panama hat, but only for the school play.

Going right over the top, beyond anything Tommy would have done, is the story "That Boy", in which William is given a free ticket for a motor coach trip when on holiday at the seaside. He gains sympathy and a free cream tea, chocolates and sweets from a sympathetic elderly lady by spinning a fantasy yarn about his family, saying his father is a drunkard who beats him and he is bullied by a cruel older brother and sister. His description of his father's visits to public houses, followed by his throwing knives and curses at William, so shocks the woman that she goes back to the hotel where William's parents are staying and tries to reason with them to give up drink and stop ill-treating the boy. The story is probably the biggest lie of William's life – but when enjoying the bountiful cream tea he had not bargained for the pay-off.

The story "William and Photography" provides a rather exaggerated description of our suffering when Mother and Aunt Richmal decided to have a studio picture taken of "the children". We were scrubbed and brushed; then I was made to wear an awful dress in white broderie anglaise, though fortunately without frills, which I loathed. The black lace-up shoes were quite inappropriate; I should have worn party shoes but presume we could not afford them – Father was away and Mother had to teach at the High School. I was only four but even at that age saw no reason to be photographed holding Tommy's hand and looking soppy, with my head on one side. I remember objecting to that pose, incredulous that the man with the camera should really think I would ever put my head sideways like that, towards Tommy.

Tommy and I: "cute" picture dictated by photographer

Eventually the photographer took my head in his hands and bent it sideways by force, the way he wanted it. Tommy was scowling and wondering whether to attack the man but Mother and Auntie promised us a really good tea if we stayed quite still and tried to look pleasant. The result was considered a success and we got our tea. But in the story "William and Photography" he was on his own, apart from a teasing audience of Ethel and a friend, and it was he who was made to put his head to one side; naturally he objected just as much as I had done. But every time the photographer arranged the pose, William moved – time and time again. The picture is a present for his godmother and after she has put it in her family album, William adorns the other pictures with a selection of pipes, cigars, tooth gaps, specs and even an Indian head-dress for the godmother's mother.

My mother was quite a good fortune-teller. She used a rather tattered book on prediction or "divination" with a pack of playing cards – not a full pack because there was nothing below a seven. Her victim shuffled and wished, then Mother laid out the cards, first in two rows of eight, followed later by another two rows. According to how the cards came out she forecast dark strangers, a letter coming by post which could bring bad news, a pleasant surprise involving money, new interests or a promotion at work, pleasurable social activities, the illness of a close friend. There were hundreds of possibilities according to the book – even a train journey with water near the railway! Of course at that time, the early 1920s, there was no mention of cars. The whole fortune-telling procedure was ridiculed by family and friends, but they always wanted her to carry on; it was her party piece for many years. Aunt Richmal loved having her fortune told and reported back on successes, with tongue in cheek. "I *did* have a letter the next day, just as you said, and it *was* from a fair-haired woman." Everyone would laugh but secretly we all took it very seriously.

So it was not surprising that in "The Fête – and Fortune", a newcomer to William's village should turn out to have this same hobby, using exactly the same system to predict the same joys and disappointments. She agrees to be the fortune-teller at a garden fête in aid of charity and in her small tent, heavily disguised as the Woman of Mystery, she dispenses the future at 2/6d a time. When an old flame arrives unexpectedly during the afternoon she needs to get away from her tent for a short while in order to talk to him. William, having already had his fortune told at her house, has a fair idea of what to do, so takes her place as the veiled Woman of Mystery. He is lucky enough to have as clients first his much-hated schoolteacher, secondly his sister Ethel and thirdly his brother Robert. To all three he issues warnings of a young boy's fatal illness, advising all three that the boy should be treated with great kindness. As a result he receives presents and VIP treatment all round.

Continuing the recurring theme of garden fêtes, another story, "William Advertises", touches on our efforts to help at charity Sales of Work at The Rookery, the squire's house at Bromley Common. We were usually allowed to sell my grandmother's home-made toffee, packed in little greaseproof bags tied at the neck with coloured ribbon. Tommy used to sell the dark treacle toffee, with green ribbon, and I sold the ordinary toffee tied with blue. We had cardboard trays holding the packs, the placards at front and back bearing the words "BUY OUR GRANNY'S HOME-MADE TOFFEE". Tommy always found it necessary to test the toffee from time to time.

In "William Advertises" the Outlaws parade at a Sale of Work with placards advertising their favourite sweet shop belonging to Mr. Moss, who is afraid of being put out of business by a new shop in the village. As usual William goes one further by sticking an advertising card on the back of the real live duke who opens the show. Fortunately he prefers the Outlaws to the boredom of the vicar's committee, so takes them out to tea. And the new shop closes down, leaving Mr. Moss triumphant.

Other Sale of Work episodes did not have such a happy ending. In a later story, "William and the White Elephant", William sells a helper's coat for one shilling, thinking it was secondhand clothing donated for sale. This is exactly what happened to Tommy. Although in the story the coat is returned by the purchaser, though not before the Outlaws become involved in complicated adventures chasing after the wrong coat, the one Tommy sold was never seen again, much to the fury of the charity helper who owned it. At that sale or another, Tommy also sold for two shillings a valuable Chinese chess set, which he thought had been left for the Bric-a-Brac stall where he was left in charge for a short while. Too late he found it had been donated to be first prize in the Raffle.

A leopard skin that Uncle Jack sent home from Africa, as a present for my mother, became the central piece in "The Leopard Hunter". In this story a very boastful acquaintance of Mr. Brown invites himself to stay with the family and bores them all with his opinions on every possible subject, including his reminiscences of big-game hunting. William puts him to the test with a leopard skin which Mr. Brown's brother has sent from Africa, so starts a rumour that a leopard has escaped from the local circus. Once it is dark he takes the skin into the garden and hides in the bushes disguised as a leopard, to frighten the visitor. We do not question how William could have managed to wrap himself in that large skin or even move with the heavy head but it makes a good story, with William forcing the terrified man to climb onto a shed roof to escape. The Brown household is much relieved when the so-called big-game hunter packs his bags the next morning and moves on, and William is suitably rewarded by his father.

Other animals beloved by Tommy arrived on the William scene. A tortoise turned up in "William and the White Cat", shortly after Richmal heard of our rapturous meeting with Tortoise Jimmy in the middle of a Kansas road. Other boys in William's life also managed to acquire tortoises from time to time.

One of Tommy's dearest wishes was to become invisible.

He felt it would open up the most exciting possibilities – as long as he could be sure of getting back to visibility. He had a favourite coat which became his cloak of invisibility; Aunt Richmal pretended he had disappeared whenever he put it on. Much to his delight she would call out, "Tommy, Tommy, where are you? Has anyone seen Tommy?" when he was standing right beside her, and Mother insisted he should *not* wear his magic coat when crossing the road. But Aunt Richmal used the idea in "William the Matchmaker", in which he pretends that his archenemy Hubert Lane has become invisible by stepping on a particular piece of grass. Unlike Tommy, Hubert was extremely upset.

Being a useful weapon, soot appears in several stories. In the early books it is put into a man's hat twice over. The first time the feat is carried out on behalf of William by some other boys who help him get revenge on an unpopular teacher but in "Enter the Sweep" William puts soot into a hat left in the front hall by an unpopular visitor – the bag of soot having been handed to William by the sweep and put to various uses. Although it was not soot that Tommy put into a visitor's hat, this idea may have been inspired by his use of a visitor's bowler hat as a temporary resting place for his tadpoles, water and all, while he searched for a more permanent jar. His tin had been leaking badly and nearly all the water had run away; and he thought the bowler looked reasonably waterproof. But then something distracted his attention in the kitchen and during his brief absence the visitor emerged into the hall and donned his hat, only to receive a trickle of water and a family of tadpoles down his face. Richmal must have thought soot better than tadpoles.

Hats feature again in "William Starts the Holidays" when he tries to grow a plant in Ethel's hat, which he paints green to improve its appearance. Tommy, in fact, tried to grow potato plants in his shoes. But they were his own shoes and he did not paint them green. It was my mother who had a passion for painting; once she started it was impossible to stop her. She even painted cups and saucers, which stuck together, and then painted the kitchen chairs to match. I was very nervous when I heard she had painted the car, for I thought the engine heat would melt it. But really it turned out very successfully, just as the man in the paintshop had said it would.

Officially Bromley Common Church is just over 12 miles from London Bridge but it seems more like 20; possibly the crow's flight, which I cannot test, is only 12 miles. Today Bromley South station is only 17 minutes nonstop from Victoria by fast train. When studying the description of trains taken by William's father "up to town", one becomes aware that he shows extreme anxiety at the thought of missing the fast train and having to take the slow train which, he complains, stops at ten stations. This was true for the Bromley-Victoria route taken by our family during the 1920s and 1930s, and there were about the same number of stations on the alternative City line. Most people in Bromley said they were "going up to town" rather than "going to London" because Bromley is so close to London; and this phrase is used in the books, which confirms the view that Richmal had Bromley in mind.

I can see now, so many years later, that I never appreciated Mr. Brown. His every remark is so biting; one can only admire his sarcastic repartee. He upstages William at every encounter, reaching the height of playful malice in "William and the White Elephant", in which his son fails to realise that a white-elephant stall is only a charity sale of secondhand goods. I wish my own father had been like Mr. Brown, although they did have one thing in common. They would both bury themselves behind the newspaper when threatened with any disagreeable activity. Even when we moved house my father was still to be seen in an empty room, bare boards and no curtains, either still in the old house or perhaps first in the new one, sitting in the only available chair, reading the newspaper and leaving everyone else to do the work. Even my mother heaved chairs, tables, bookshelves and heavy cartons about the place; but my father continued to read the paper.

There was a marked similarity between Mrs Brown and my mother: both tended to remain calm in circumstances that would drive most women to hysterics. They both believed the best of their sons and, although apprehensive of the disasters that were likely, they still believed that one day the son would grow into a respectable citizen. Mrs Brown was slightly more placid than my mother, perhaps because her husband was more reliable and there were no financial crises apart from William's continuous shortage of funds. Family and visitors were constantly bringing dramatic tidings of William's

101

activities, and all she did was change the colour of the wool for the socks she was darning. It was the cook rather than Mrs Brown who bellowed at William. His mother was his very best friend, a fact that William never realised. It took Tommy a long time to appreciate *his* mother's qualities, but eventually he did understand; and at last they grew into old age together almost like Darby and Joan.

VII

Our Spiritual Home – The Glebe

The house is still there – the beautiful house now mellowed, with greenery growing up the walls. Returning as a nostalgic observer I see that new owners have added two more garages, cut down some of the trees and put up a large notice: WARNING – DOGS LOOSE. The blue plaque by the front door states that Richmal Crompton, Authoress, lived here from 1928 to 1954 and one of the bricks by the front door is carved with her initials: RCL 1927. There is no mention of William. I creep up the short drive, waiting for the dogs to spring from nowhere. This was for a while my home – The Glebe.

I had watched every stage of the building, from the foundations almost to the last brick. RCL did not merely live at The Glebe; she had bought the land and commissioned the building, while Clara had directed the architects, telling them exactly what to do. The house was to have a Queen Anne look, and to embrace four rooms upstairs and three at ground level. Clara refused to accept the architects' plans for the kitchen and scullery, wanting them much more spacious. She took great care to select the best position for Richmal's study and had very definite ideas about the staircase, because she knew Richmal would have difficulty with too many steps at a time. On the landings she wanted to find the right settings for the African spears and framed Chinese embroideries brought home by Jack as presents.

Although the garden was only an acre it was to us, possibly owing to its length, a vast landscape with dense woodlands. A deep shrubbery ran all down one side. At first it was wild and untamed, thick with trees and tangled undergrowth – our very own forest, where no human had ever set foot before. Tommy, then 12, and his friend Peter Freeman cleared a route through the jungle, which they regarded as secret, known only to themselves. Unfortunately they disturbed a hornets' nest and were quite badly stung.

Long before the house was finished they could make camp fires, track wild animals and climb trees without the risk of enraged farmers chasing them away. Several old and solid trees in the front of the house, to some extent hidden from the road, added to the adventure. From the higher branches – easily climbed by the boys – the road could be kept under observation. Fields round three sides of the garden gave protection from interference, like a moat. The nearest big house was the Holy Trinity vicarage, typically old and rambling, where the Reverend Mr. Gompertz lived. All down the opposite side of the road were woods and fields, inhabited only by a few farm sheds and a small farmhouse and today still miraculously preserved in a green state right up to Barnet Wood Road.

Our spiritual home – The Glebe – with new driveway

We all made frequent inspections of The Glebe's construction. Tommy would walk the planks and climb the ladders when the workmen were out of sight. I took a snapshot of Aunt Richmal at the official laying of the brick with her initials, placed into the partly built frontage at a time when the building was still in a state of chaos. There was an exact description of the site in the story "William Adopts an Orphan", published the next year.

The Glebe is almost alongside the group of small houses

and shops on either side of the Two Doves public house, halfway along Oakley Road. In 1928 the butcher, shoemaker, linen draper, greengrocer-cum-general store and the tobacconist-sweet shop formed a self-contained domain. The draper is now a general store and all the others have been converted into rather smart little cottages. One of the most attractive, with wooden balcony, was our sweet shop and

Photo: Doreen Spooner

Our HQ, the Oakley Road sweetshop, now residential

another characterful cottage in white clapboard was the original general store. In the summer, huge bunches of blue wisteria still hang from a tree climbing up the front and side of the aptly named Wisteria Cottage. The Two Doves remains the centrepiece and landmark, being the Oakley Road stop for the Bromley-Westerham buses.

During the last part of the 19th century there had been several other "beer retailers" and even a local brewery. But such establishments were not on our visiting list and the Two Doves was completely out of bounds, as was the Bird in Hand nearby on the corner of Cross Road and Gravel Road, a present-day local meeting place. Up until the war, the Lamburn family took for granted that public houses were for workmen; the only references to pubs in the early William books related to tramps.

Our headquarters in Oakley Road – the sweet shop – was well stocked with liquorice strips curled into tight whirls, the harder liquorice sticks, the famous all-sorts and little packs of sherbert which could be sucked up through a straw. Acid drops, which made a funny feeling down the sides of my face, and fruit drops were cheaper than bullseyes and peppermint lumps. Penny bars of milk chocolate were equally popular and there was a dark red fizzy drink called Valencia, rather too sweet but more powerful than ginger beer. Cheap strong lemonade could be made from packets of powder they sold.

Apart from The Glebe, my grandmother Clara had two more spiritual homes: the department stores Medhurst's in Bromley and the Army & Navy in London. We made occasional family pilgrimages to that Victoria Street shrine of retail service to the officer classes (at that time no post orders were accepted from the other ranks); we would have lunch there before going on to a theatre, usually a musical. Clara liked being early, partly to set us a good example, so we were made to arrive everywhere half an hour before anything was due to start. We waited on empty station platforms, in restaurant foyers before the doors opened and half an hour at a time in empty theatres. It gave me great pain to waste so much of my life in this way.

Clara held court at coffee time every Saturday morning in Medhurst's restaurant. All available members of the family were expected to attend after shopping in the town. During term time the party was reduced to Clara, Richmal and my mother, with the addition of Uncle Jack when he was living at The Glebe or nearby after he married. My diaries show that the coffee sessions often produced small cash handouts, always welcome, usually several shillings. Whenever there were visitors to The Glebe they joined us.

William had aunts and great-aunts galore but no uncles that I remember and – in all those years – only one glimpse of a grandfather and no grandmother at all. William would have loved Clara, though he would perhaps have found her strictness a problem. She might have made him wash his hands too often and, even worse, demanded complete punctuality. Tommy tried to look neat and tidy in her presence and indeed all photographs show him looking swept and polished, but it never lasted long. His hair was curly and wild, going its own way most of the time. It would keep flat for half an hour when plastered down with water – unlike mine, which was horribly straight anyway.

Tommy aged 10

Although Clara was a teetotaller she made wonderful wines, which she left to mature in The Glebe's attic. Potato, apple, raspberry and rhubarb worked out best and they proved exceedingly potent – as we found out when we reached our teens and sampled them to celebrate birthdays and other festive occasions. The attic also contained her home-made jams and bottled fruits, all carefully labelled and date-marked. William might have raided the attic and held a Sale of these goodies but we never did. It was Clara's special province. Richmal liked sherry and wines but knowing that drink was "in the family", she was always careful.

In those days Clara had an easy time with all the domestic shopping; everything was delivered from the local Bromley Common shops, some only a few hundred yards away. The butcher, baker, greengrocer and milkman all called regularly; we knew their staff well, having a genuine interest in their successes and failures, their illnesses, births, deaths and marriages. A few weeks after the butcher's assistant's wedding, Richmal asked her how she liked married life. "Oh, it's all right," she said. "But isn't it *rude*." Richmal was taken aback by the comment but on finding that it amused Clara, she retold it many times later.

It was during the early days at The Glebe that Tommy decided to help Clara. She had been rash enough to remark, "There is no one left to call me Clara. I am 'Mother' or 'Granny' or 'Mrs Lamburn' but the people who called me Clara are either dead or live hundred of miles away." Tommy thought this extremely sad. "*We* will call you Clara," he promised and the next morning set out early to look for the milkman, waylaying him before his morning's call. They appeared to be having a very earnest conversation and we were horrified a few minutes later to hear the milkman say, "Good morning, Clara! Any cream today?" We expected an angry rebuff but on the contrary, she loved it. Gradually more

Tea at The Glebe: Clara, Richmal, Peter and Tommy

people did the same, prompted by Tommy. Aunt Richmal sometimes introduced her to visitors as "my mother, Clara". Tommy and I used to call her Donna Clara, after the popular song of the time. Tommy sang loudly all over the house: "Oh, Donna Claara, I saw you dancing tonight. Oh, Donna Claara – you bee-long to mee." We were not quite sure of the other words.

Clara's children and her daily maid Kathleen did not join the Friends of Clara. Kathleen was rather shocked by such disrespect. It was owing to her faithful presence that Richmal and Clara could entertain people to lunch, tea, for drinks – whatever suited friends travelling from London to Bromley Common, often met by Richmal at Bromley South station. She gradually widened her circles of friends and acquaintances, often through educational and literary contacts which started from fan mail. People recognised by her use of the English language (with many obscure and erudite words) and frequent classical references in the William stories – though obviously not spoken by William himself – that this was an educated authoress, not merely a writer of children's books.

In the mid-1920s Aunt Richmal had been excited to find that adjustments could be made to cars; hand controls could replace foot pedals for acceleration and braking. If she bought a car she could become mobile, without being dependent any more on friends and taxis. She bought her first car about 1927 and with the move to The Glebe a few months later, it could be safely garaged. Yet she must have found long car journeys too tiring for she usually went by train to the South Coast holiday resorts that Clara liked so much. They chose the most conventional places – Eastbourne, Bournemouth and Hove were favourites. Sometimes we stayed near them, in the same town. Clara liked all the large grand hotels with marble pillars; we could only afford the humbler boarding houses but kept ourselves free for meals in the marble halls and tea amidst the palms. Richmal never went back to Cromer, where she had developed polio; and mention of the town was always avoided by the rest of the family.

During our childhood and teenage years, Jack was our hero. I thought him handsome and romantic and noticed that whenever he was due home on leave there was increased interest in the Lamburn family on the part of the local girls, who were all quite old by our standards. Norah Harris of Oakley Farm near The Glebe had always been on very friendly terms with Clara and Richmal, and could walk into the house at any time, often bringing new-laid eggs; but when Jack was home she seemed to come much more frequently. The elder sister of a school friend of mine was known to be buying a lot of new clothes; I was told the reason – Jack – by my friend under oath of secrecy which, I am sure, can be broken now.

But Jack remained a bachelor for a long time and we never had any clues about relationships he might have formed in Africa and China. His other adventures were enough for us and the presents he brought back for Clara, Richmal and Gwen were unusual and exciting. For many years I remained on hugging terms with a leopard he had shot in his early hunting days. He had presented my mother with the complete skin mounted on felt: paws and tail spread out and the great head showing teeth bared in an angry snarl. We were allowed to play hunt the leopard indoors but Tommy wanted to take it outside to show his friends, which my mother would never allow. She used it as a hearth rug and we all tripped over its head: so one afternoon she solved the problem by chopping it into several pieces, keeping the body for the fireside. I was so upset I took charge of the head and paws; I cannot remember what happened to the tail. The head came in useful as a hatstand, for in those days all "nice" young ladies wore hats and gloves. I stitched the two long paws down the back of a coat, starting at the shoulders and meeting at the waist, enjoying the idea of frightening anyone following me in the dark.

In his letters to my mother Jack mesmerised us with tales of Shanghai and Hong Kong, where he spent some of his shorter leaves. For me his most exciting adventure was the train journey right across Russia, the Trans-Siberian route starting in China, and his description of Lenin on display in Moscow. We boasted to our friends, "My uncle has seen the dead body of Lenin." But luck was against me when eventually I explored Moscow. The tomb was closed for spring-cleaning.

The Glebe served as a home for Jack when he retired early and returned to England. In his late thirties and still unmarried, he lived for a while with Clara and Richmal at Bromley Common. He had already started writing novels based on his African adventures and in 1931 *Trooper Fault* was published under the name John Lambourne. He continued the African theme with other books, described by one critic as a cross between Haggard, Wells and Kipling. In 1933 he married a young widow – Joan Cooke, whom he had met while on holiday in Birchington – and moved to a house of his own, where he continued to write, keeping bees as a hobby.

Newly engaged Jack Lamburn and Joan Cooke, with Richmal

My own favourite amongst Jack's books, *The Kingdom That Was*, published by John Murray in 1931 (with a second imprint 40 years later, just before his death), also appeared in shortened form in *Reader's Digest*. It was then selected by Gerald du Maurier for filming but, sadly, du Maurier's death put a stop to the project. Jack went back to the study of insects, though to his regret without the same wealth of material available in Africa and China. From this time onwards he wrote about nature and animals under the name John Crompton – completely different in style from his previous books – starting with *A Hive of Bees*, then *The Hunting Wasp, The Spider, Ways of the Ant* and others, bringing the total to 15. Now, nearly a century after his birth, some of these books are being republished in the USA. It has been said that they are enthralling, bringing the creatures to life as no text book has ever managed to do. Richmal, Clara and Gwen were, of course, delighted with Jack's success and there were many family gatherings and celebrations with Jack,

Joan and their son David, born in 1934.

David became the next small boy in the family for Richmal to study. When Jack, accompanied by his family, returned to The Glebe for a while during the last years of the war, David was by then the appropriate age of 10. His sister Sarah, born in 1944, has three sons, the youngest called William. He is Richmal's great-nephew (born 7 years after her death) who reached the age of 14 in the year of her Centenary – 1990. In between David and William, there had been my sister's son Edward, of 1954 vintage, who was able to update Richmal's knowledge of boys in the 1960s.

Apart from his books, Jack wrote regular articles for *Blackwood's* magazine and *John Bull*, and when Richmal felt she was running out of ideas for William stories in the late 1940s he offered to help; over a period of several years he provided several plots and other contributions for a number of the William books.

Although from time to time Richmal said that incidents in Jack's childhood had provided ideas for William stories, he always denied having been a William-type character. In later years he told his son David that he could not have risked either his father's disapproval or any embarrassment for his mother. In any event, we all knew that his personality was completely different from William's – Jack was a gentler and altogether more sensitive type of person. William's basic problem was that he could never forsee the probable result of his actions, which was more typical of Tommy than Jack.

One of Jack's achievements as a schoolboy was to flick a pat of butter onto the ceiling by putting it on the tip of a knife and using the blade as a catapault. When I unashamedly tried the same thing at boarding school, I had to pay for the whole of the ceiling being repainted. Unfortunately it had landed above a tea urn and the steam – over a period of time – caused it to melt and spread. It was a term and a half before the staff noticed, although everyone else knew what I had done, and the outcome was rather expensive. All the same, it was a very satisfying experience.

Although The Glebe was the best-loved house of my life, especially during the 1930s, I did not move into it completely until the 1939 war was imminent, when we packed up our possessions and joined Auntie Ray, for mutual support.

VIII

The Return of Father

When Father went back to Tahiti for the winter of 1923/4 he left Mother with insufficient funds, so she applied rather desperately to the two managers in charge of the businesses, principally the Per Mundum Tour agency in Camberwell.

One of them replied: "I realised that the amount he left you would not be sufficient to take you through until his return, so have written to know what he proposes to allow you whilst away, as I fully expect you will need some more money before he returns. It will be very difficult for you, but I dare not voice an opinion on the matter. I shall however chat to Mr. Disher about it on his return. Really I feel he does not quite realise how troublesome it is with two young children at times. He is away so much that he sees little of them, and is apt to overlook the responsibility entailed on their account. I trust, Mrs Disher, that you will pardon my mentioning this, but it does not seem quite right that you should have to seek employment with two young children to look after. If you are in want of any advice or help, please let us know, and we will do whatever we can to assist you."

But letters to and from Tahiti took a long time and in the end the managers could do nothing to help financially. At that time Aunt Richmal was only just recovering from polio and was having a difficult time supporting herself and Clara. But Mother was lucky enough to find a small house in a short cul-de-sac near Mason's Hill, an easy bus or cycle ride to Bromley Common. A row of six semi-detached houses formed a hidden 'Avenue', as it was rather grandly named, generally free of traffic except for the milkman's cart, delivery boys on bicycles and the occasional repair van. None of the residents owned cars, though some of their visitors were more affluent.

Fortunately Oakwood Avenue was not far from Bromley High School, where Mother and Auntie had been teaching. A passageway led to a long iron bridge spanning the four railway platforms of Bromley South Station, and steps down the far side came out in Elmfield Road, almost at the entrance to the High School. So it was only a five-minute walk for students to come to the house for special coaching. Possibly my mother had this in mind when selecting the house. Her degree subjects – mathematics, English and French – were fortunately much in demand, but it was often a case of "Shssh – Mother's doing her homework."

The railway bridge was the perfect vantage point for train spotting, but Tommy and his friends needed action and got bored with so much waiting around. They could reach the town centre, the Market Place, through a long narrow path fenced on either side most of the way, called Love Lane, which led from the bridge steps along the back of the town.

1920. Bromley Market in action

The market was held every Thursday and provided many delights, from barrel organs with tame monkeys to birds in cages and talking parrots. Rabbits and other pets were for sale but we were usually held back by financial problems. Tommy was entranced by the sales patter of the market-stall owners, which he used to imitate at home. They learned to bar his way when he appeared, to ward off his unflattering comments and constant heckling, which caused potential customers to drift away. He wanted to expose their incorrect statements and warn the small crowds that gathered. Or so he said. The more friendly marketeers taught him the lingo – "Speak to me softly" meant "Quote lowest possible price". There were other mystifying statements with hidden meaning.

Tommy was by now avoiding my company, not wanting to be seen with a girl; and from then on he preferred his own gang of boys from the local County School where he had been accepted. I did not mind; they were often noisy and rough, always fighting and getting into difficulties with the school authorities and sometimes the police. But I did rather like two brothers called Sherriff. There were other children in the neighbourhood so I was never lonely, and in due course I was sent to the High School.

I suffered most from Tommy's collection of caterpillars, which lived in a series of small cages. There were some that looked dreadful, with terrifying faces even square-shaped, and others with tiny horns. When Tommy wanted to frighten me he would say that some had escaped. I always believed him and frantically searched every inch of my room, stripping the bed layer by layer, then passing a restless night. When they really did escape, the house had to be turned inside out to find them. Any visitors were warned off the upholstered chairs in case the pests lurked in hidden folds; he was most anxious that the creatures should not be hurt. We all wanted to see them back under lock and key. It was my job to collect poplar leaves and nettles for their food, and once they turned into chrysalises we knew that they would soon become butterflies. Tommy used to put twigs into the little cages, and once the chrysalis had split he would take the twig and emerging butterfly into the garden, which was an exciting moment.

We were used to Tommy dashing into the hedgerows shouting, "It's a Red Admiral!" as he chased butterflies to study their markings and colours. Among his other special favourites were the Peacock, Purple Emperor, Painted Lady, Swallowtail and Tortoiseshell. All their eggs, caterpillars and chrysalises were different shapes and colours. I wanted to see the caterpillars eat their own shells after hatching but my timing was never right. Tommy showed me the skins they kept shedding like snakes. Some caterpillars were striped black and yellow; they had real legs at the front and false legs at the back. Although repelled by them, I could see the fascination – except when they emerged from his pockets and crawled up his sleeves.

Sometimes I was allowed to join the moth-collecting expeditions into the woods. It was only occasionally that they needed my help and even then merely in a subsidiary role. Tommy would make a mixture of honey and beer, put it in empty jam jars he had saved, and then – armed with torches, a roll of paper, some string and a spoon or two – we would set out for the woods as soon as it was dark. With his two friends Peter and Frank, Tommy would choose a tree in a suitable clearing, fasten the paper round the trunk, then spread the honey and beer mix all over it. We'd stand two or three yards away, shining our torches onto the band of intoxicating honey. In a short while the moths would come, attracted first by the light and then by the smell; eventually they'd go too near, getting stuck to the band like flies. Tommy would gently pull them away, dropping them into his killing bottle. Back at home he mounted them onto card, with the species identified, dealing with their dead bodies and wings as calmly as he mounted stamps into albums.

I never stopped to wonder what death-gas was in the bottle and even now have no idea. It was all very exciting and I was proud to be included; though on reflection, it seems extraordinary for a boy who loved insects to kill them in this way. I have been asked how they got the beer but it was not difficult for boys passing the tables outside a pub to capture the dregs left in glasses. It was more difficult to get the honey, for pocket money was scarce, and beehives are not known to be friendly.

In daytime he looked for his favourite owls, which were asleep. The white-faced barn owls looked lovely but screeched wildly when he approached. I was entranced by the ones that hooted softly, the brown owls, which preferred to nest in the trees. He collected their coughed-up pellets to see what they had eaten that day, which I thought disgusting. Usually they had swallowed, whole, some of his friends – the mice.

Fund-raising was always a serious matter. There was a

limit to the tips we were likely to get from grown-ups and our pocket money was small. It was essential to earn money somehow. If other people could do it, we could too. First we tried selling playing cards for a penny but only the court cards had sufficient consumer appeal. We bound the edges with black sticky tape called passe-partout, which was all the rage at that time. Tommy's fingers were too clumsy so I had to take over the edging. His sales efforts were unsuccessful so I stood alone at the corner of a street in Bromley, where I knew the men would be coming home from work. I did quite a reasonable trade, running out of stock quite quickly. If we could have sold all 52 cards, we could have replaced them and made a profit; the one and threepence we did earn would have been useful but it failed to compensate for the row over the pack now without its more colourful characters. We were accused of begging and of being an embarrassment to the family. If we had begged for a penny for the guy, as they do today, I could have seen the point. But we were trying our hand at the manufacturing process, which today would be called enterprise. I resolved another time to use a disguise, for a neighbour had told Mother what we were doing.

Tommy tried odd jobs such as weeding someone's allotment, with obvious results and no cash. He washed Auntie's car – both inside and out – but was too overcome with remorse to accept payment. Messenger services were a better proposition, because few people had telephones. The Boy Scouts seemed to have taken over all the paid odd-jobs and although Tommy was a Crusader there was no money in it – quite the reverse. They wanted money from us. With so many horses around, it is surprising that we never thought of a trade in manure.

Our summer holidays, usually spent near Clara and Richmal, provided scope for adventure. Margate, for instance, had a permanent funfair called Dreamland but whereas the beach and sea were free, Dreamland was expensive. Tommy lived in hopes of winning prizes, at the very least coconuts, which could then be sold for a profit to be reinvested in more competitions, resulting in more prizes. For some unknown reason, this perfectly good theory never worked out in practice. Other problems followed us. When he tried to help a young shoeshine boy who worked at our hotel, Tommy got up early and collected the shoes from outside the guests' rooms but forgot to chalk the room number of the sole of each shoe. He tried to correct the situation when he returned them, but his arbitrary pairing of male and female shoes outside the doors led to some obvious complications in the morning, and Tommy had to admit his errors in order to defend the shoe boy.

Other troubles arose over Tommy's lost clothes. He always knew exactly where he had left them on the beach and accused innocent people of theft, only to find the clothes hours later somewhere else, half buried in sand. In the books, William also had a tendency to lose his clothes. The Browns' bill for William's clothing must have been horrendous. Even his best suits, complete with waistcoats, were stolen by tramps or exchanged for more exotic garb, or damaged beyond repair by coatings of cement, frequent immersion in ponds, ditches and streams or else torn to shreds. Tommy did not go that far. His losses were merely caps, socks, shoes, ties, sweaters and of course garters and shoelaces.

At home most of Tommy's activities were well away from the Avenue, because it offered no escape route. The chase stopped there. Policemen who followed him home found there were only six houses to call on. Their bicycle tyres could become inexplicably flat even while they were interviewing Mother, but she developed a technique of admiration and sympathy which helped to calm them down. She was, of course, wary of every knock on the door; although it was more likely to be an irate neighbour than the police, who generally had more serious crimes to investigate. She could deal with school authorities but her real lifelong fear was of an ambulance. Yet when it arrived, it came for her.

It is remarkable how many times William climbed through windows – in nearly every story. Being an expert, he could master any style of window yet was often lucky enough to find an easy route up a tree and over a roof. With a monkey-like agility he could get through larder windows and garden-shed skylights with little damage to his person, though much to his clothes. He could have grown into an excellent cat burglar. Tommy, on the other hand, had no such ability; he was strong but rather clumsy and could be guaranteed to break the window latch if not the glass. He had discovered at an early age that glass was a ridiculously weak substance. Doors served him no better because he never understood that a handle could be turned and a door shut quietly, so he gave away his presence nearly every time.

Tommy was not the only window-climber in the family. My mother occasionally locked herself out of the house and had to find another way in. One time she broke her wrist climbing through a rather high kitchen window and was taken to Bromley Hospital to have it X-rayed and set in plaster. As the other wrist was receiving wax treatment for arthritis at Beckenham Hospital she found herself with each wrist registered in a different hospital three miles apart. All our efforts to get the left wrist transferred to the right or vice versa failed dismally owing to red tape. Fortunately it turned out that the one wrist was not, after all, arthritic and the other healed up in time.

During these years, when we were invited to children's parties grown-ups started identifying us as Just William and his sister, which spoiled everything. It was as if they expected us to behave badly, which we hated and did not understand. When they fussed over us, asking about Auntie, the other children thought we were out of the zoo. Fancy-dress parties were better, when we were safely disguised. Mother spent hours making special outfits without spending much cash. She was clever with her hands and quite a good artist. She played the piano, too – often at night just as we were drifting off to sleep.

Mother in her forties

During one of my father's annual returns to Europe, in the mid 1920s, we were taken for one more trip abroad, this time to France. We stayed for several weeks at the vast Hotel Regina just outside Nice, now a hospital. Both parents caught the gambling bug trying their luck in Monte Carlo. For a while our paternal grandparents were with us as guests of the Per Mundum Tours, which used the hotel as a base. This left our parents free to gamble the night away, or at any rate the evenings. Mother was very successful, which was a blow to the financial wizard's pride. So he brought back to England all the recorded results of the past weeks and months, and arranged to have the future gaming results posted to him when available. There were times when every inch of the main rooms of our house was covered with these record sheets which must not be touched while he tried to work out a mathematical formula that would give him a foolproof answer. It never surfaced.

Father kept two very powerful cars in the south of France, to drive small parties of tourists up to the small mountain villages such as Grasse, famous for perfume, and sometimes right over the Alps, taking Napoleon's route. On a family trip we stopped to pick armfuls of lavender, which Tommy and I tried unsuccessfully to turn to financial advantage; but we were told to give it away as presents. I must have developed my love of mountains and lakes there and in Switzerland, a landscape which left Tommy unmoved. He preferred the sea and the beaches. At that time Juan-les-Pins was only a tiny village, with very shallow water going out a long way before it became at all deep, and our parents thought this the safest beach.

We preferred Cannes; it was more exciting and I managed to earn a French franc in a most curious way. I was trotting down to the beach on my own, tired of waiting for Mother and Tommy, when a strange man offered to show me the sea – which seemed rather silly, considering it was right in front of us. But my understanding of French was not very good and I thought he must have come from Mother, until he led me down a narrow side passage running between tall buildings. He stopped, looked up at the walls, which had very few windows, picked me up and started kissing me and feeling me all over, which struck me as an odd thing for a complete stranger to do. Suddenly – at the sound of men's footsteps approaching – he put me down, handed me a franc and ran away. Meanwhile Mother was starting to search the beach. "Look what I've got," I said triumphantly and Tommy was envious. Then a lot of time was wasted at a police station where they all talked very fast in French, including Mother. Afterwards she declared Cannes to be "out of bounds" for us and in compensation took us by boat to the nearby island of St Marguerite.

In Paris we did the tourist sights – the Eiffel Tower and the Louvre – and also played in the Tuileries Gardens. I have a feeling that at that age we would have preferred Robinson, the small town south of Paris now reached on a suburban rail line, where there are houses and a restaurant built up in the trees, which I found forty years later. But Versailles was brought to life for us by Mother's enthusiasm for Louis XVI's court and the Marie Antoinette story. The Revolution fired Tommy's imagination but I remained firmly on the other side. I was a Royalist; he could have the other lot, including Napoleon. We had some very confused ideas of history which Mother tried patiently to correct. "No, darling, Napoleon was *not* murdered in his bath. Robespierre did *not* beome King or Emperor."

The best part of Paris was for us the pavement cafés. We wanted the crown corks from the bottles, scattered on the ground all round the tables. We got down on hands and knees, stuffing them in our pockets. Tommy crawled under neighbouring tables until the other people began to complain when his curly head emerged from under the tablecloths. Father hauled him back. "What *are* you doing, Tommy? Get up off the pavement. Now your hands and knees are filthy." Our parents apologised all round. I can still hear Father's reproaches. But he did not understand, and we could not tell him in case he stopped us, that the corks were going be our fleet.

Back at the hotel we were going to fight the French at Trafalgar. All we needed now was a few matchsticks and some stiff paper. The difficult part was to slice the matchsticks downwards, to hold the paper sails; after that it was easy to plant this mast into the centre of the cork. I flatly refused to hold the matchsticks while Tommy slit them with a penknife, but it could be done quite easily by laying them flat. The match head then had to be chopped off. Moving to the nearest bathroom, we blew the fleets into position; but most of the ships capsized and sank, so had to be dried out and fitted with new sails. We took turns to be Nelson. And as far as we were concerned Paris could keep the Louvre, with all those dreary pictures and statues.

All my life father conducted a campaign against smoking and drinking – even tea and coffee. To him they were all drugs. He appeared to be keen on natural living, with all that it implied. My mother's surreptitious smoking was to him a constant source of annoyance, for she and Richmal had smoked since their thirties. From Father's point of view, Mother had replied to his advertisement for a nonsmoking teetotal secretary when she was 25 and she had no right to change her mode of living now. He could break the marriage vows but she could not even smoke . . . Then a doctor friend advised him that chewing gum could have the same effect as smoking so, always wholesale-minded, Father bought a gross of Wrigley's chewing-gum packs. It was not a good decision because for weeks afterwards he found parked gum everywhere he went – on chairs and tables, the banisters, the hall coatstand and in the bathroom. But Tommy and I had a wonderful time and were disappointed when the gross was not replenished.

Home entertainment and card games were important to all families in those pre-television days. We were taught auction bridge before I was eight and chess soon afterwards. Later the others took up contract bridge but I was bored by the way they analysed every hand afterwards, reproaching each other for not having led with this or that. Then there were whist drives, with local enthusiasts invited home and children made to keep out of the way. So we held our own whist drives, with

our own friends, making our own rules. I bought a chess set with ten shillings Uncle Jack had sent for Christmas and kept it for years until we were told to give games to the troops fighting abroad during the war. My lifelong love affair with trains can be traced back to another purchase with Jack's Christmas money – my precious Hornby train set.

Father did not believe in presents, saying they were a waste of money. In the 1920s and 30s his financial status was as

Tommy at prep school, aged 13

volatile as the stock market. On Mondays, Wednesdays and Fridays he was a millionaire but on Tuesdays, Thursdays and Saturdays he was on the verge of bankruptcy, or so it seemed to us. It was impossible to know whether we could afford anything. One day it was Yes, the next day No. In any case he could probably get it wholesale if we waited – usually in vain. He bought many different businesses, sometimes merely stripping the assets, at other times putting the previous management again in charge and trying to build it up. He must have been one of the first to adopt a policy of diversification; his interests in the UK alone ranged from pickles to quarries.

After several years at Bromley County School it was obvious that Tommy was getting nowhere academically. He had played truant too often and although not expelled he was quietly moved to a prep school nearby – St Hugh's in Bickley – where he became a boarder and could be kept under stricter control. As usual, Auntie paid the bills. He soon learned that the honour of the school was at stake any time he was wearing the school cap, whose badge was well known locally, for the donning of caps was now compulsory. Mother and Auntie were delighted that he found an outlet for his energy in sports, especially boxing, rugger and swimming.

Only very recently have I realised that my father probably registered his domicile abroad during these years of wandering, in the hope of avoiding UK taxes. He moved his official base from time to time; at the last stage I think it was in the Bahamas. Or perhaps that was a holding company. No one could ever quite follow what he was doing. Eventually he must have lost a lot of money; I always thought a small part would have been better used repaying Aunt Richmal for Tommy's education. She had given us so much financial help over the years but she never said a word of reproach and he never ever thanked her. At least he had paid for my education, opening a bank account from which I paid my school fees and living expenses during term time. No doubt I was a director of one of his many companies; no agreement or signature seems to have been needed at that time and so I would not have known.

IX

Civilising the Teenagers

It was time for us to become responsible citizens, to obey the laws of the land and honour those elected to positions of authority. With a little bit of luck, Tommy's sporting prowess would overshadow his lack of academic ability and get him into a public school. It had happened often enough and Cheltenham proved no exception. The prep school gave him a good report; Aunt Richmal paid the fees and he remained at Cheltenham from 1927 to 1933. Then, having failed in School Certificate, he was taken away and sent to a private "crammer" in Norfolk, where Aunt Richmal hoped a second opportunity early in 1934 would prove more successful. Unfortunately the results were no better, although he had learned to play golf and appreciate the local girls.

In the summer of 1928 I took the entrance exam for Cheltenham Ladies' College. Both my mother and Aunt Richmal went with me for the interview. I had in fact refused to go back to Bromley High School one weekday in the summer term, after a stormy session with the headmistress. She had accused me of being a gang leader, of copying heroines in popular girls' school books, and asked if I read Angela Brazil. I had never heard the name before but assumed it was recommended reading – some good literary work – and so answered "Yes." It was the wrong answer; apparently this author was regarded as a bad influence. So I was given a real dressing-down although, said my tormentor, it grieved her to speak to me this way, especially because my mother and aunt had both given such excellent service to the school.

That autumn term I started my seven-year career in one of the strictest girls' boarding schools in the country. Although Tommy was at the boys' school in the same town, we were never allowed to meet. Being considered evil, boys were not permitted to walk the same streets as the girls. They had the High Street but we had The Promenade, which was wide and tree-lined – much more attractive. All the lesser streets were allocated in the same way, so that never the twain should meet. Our College buildings were in the centre, near The

Prom, with the boarding houses spread out through different parts of the town. Roughly 100 pupils were day girls, the remaining 700-800 being boarders. I was in St Austin's House, very close to the College.

The regime was not unlike that of St Elphins, where Aunt Richmal and Mother had been boarders; but whereas the girls at St Elphins had at that time all been Church of England clergy daughters, at Cheltenham we had a mixture of religions and a few other races, including one of the Ethiopian royals. I have amusing memories of two Indian sisters who spoke English perfectly (better than the rest of us) and who taught me how to tie a sari, an art I have since lost through lack of practice. It came in useful for decorating the statues that were dotted here and there, the sari being a far more exciting outfit than some of the bizarre underwear we had previously used. We teased the Indians about strange ceremonies we said they conducted behind locked doors, standing in basins full of water, with chamber pots on their heads. In return they deliberately led us on, with chanting, wailing and ghostly shrieks – all with good humour. In fact, we knew they were Christians.

We were made to work hard and play games with determination and energy; this was – I think – partly to keep our minds off the forbidden subject. It was very difficult to find out anything in that direction but the girls with older brothers were expected to be better informed than most and many of them spread horror stories of what we could expect in adult life. Having an older brother I was regarded as a possible authority, although in fact Tommy had told me very little. On Sundays we were supposed to read Good Books so this became our day for studying the Bible, identifying passages that provided interesting clues. There was everything – detective stories, murder, incest, sodomy and frequent references to what we concluded made the world go round. We found it was possible to converse in Biblical code. The only one I remember – Amos 3:3 – was almost a declaration of war, reading when decoded "Can two walk together except they be agreed?"

In the holidays Tommy and I used to make our plans to meet during the Sunday afternoon walks the following term. The route depended on the time of year and the weather. Cheltenham Ladies always walked in crocodile formation, closely chaperoned, until reaching a more countrified area, where file could be broken before returning to "croc" once again in the town. I was careful to be friendly with the maids, then messages could be got out, even letters posted. If it had been easy to meet we would not have bothered but the difficulties made it dangerous and exciting. I never knew whether he had received the route message until his head popped up from the bushes or he dropped from a tree, much to the horror of our escorts. "It's only my brother," I would say, but as there was no resemblance between us, new staff were not sure whether to believe me. They could neither send him away nor make me disappear, so they clung to us like leeches. By the time we had exchanged enough news about home, Mother, Auntie Ray and Clara, they realised I was speaking the truth.

From time to time Clara and Auntie paid us state visits; only then was Tommy allowed on The Prom. They used to stay at the imposing Queen's Hotel nearby, which had the necessary marble pillars for Clara. But the teas there were much too dull, so we went to a spacious café in The Prom that catered for junior appetites. On Saturdays in term time it was full of visiting parents and their offspring, all eating ice-cream sundaes running with sticky sauces, topped with huge mounds of whipped cream and pieces of rare fruits. Poor William, how he would have loved that café – but he was stuck in his village, with only an occasional outing. Sometimes we kept him a spare chair.

It was in the Christmas holidays after my first term at Cheltenham that I realised – and was then told – that Mother was "expecting". She explained that she and Father thought it was a good idea to have another baby. I refrained from saying she was a bit too old for that sort of thing; after all, she was on the verge of 40. There was obviously nothing I could do about it and anyway I would be back at school when it happened. Mother was sure it would be a boy; he would be called Arthur after one of Aunt Ada's sons killed in the war. From then on we referred to the bump as Arthur but in the event, early in March the next year, it turned out to be a girl and she was christened Richmal, after our aunt, great-aunt, mother's cousin and our great-grandmother. Within the family the various Richmals had been called Ray, Re or Rene and so we had to call this one by her name in full because Rye

– all that was left – sounded too much like cockney for Ray.

The house in the cul-de-sac avenue was now far too small. It had been the right size in 1924 for Mother, Tommy and me, with Father there sometimes for a month or two at a time; but now there were three children and Father was no longer spending the winters in Tahiti – we had to move. The next house, in Plaistow Lane at Sundridge Park, a residential area to the north of Bromley, had a third floor which provided spacious attic rooms for Tommy's hobbies. By now they comprised caterpillar-breeding, goldfish, minnow and stickleback colonies with weeds, newts, various types of beetle, supplies of plants for inmates of the insect zoo and the occasional tame mouse, which had to be kept apart or it would have made short work of its companions. There were albums and packets of stamps, a boxing punchball, paint, football and rugger boots, to which later he added a few golf clubs, balls, tees, etc. And now there was space in the house for a live-in mother's help-cum-nurse to help with the baby.

Yet this final effort of Mother's to save the marriage failed. She was accustomed to Father's incurable womanising, for in the early days of their marriage he had told her that no woman could resist him. Now he wanted power over people and tried to dominate everyone in the family and his businesses. But he was up against Aunt Richmal. Twice he upset Mother so much that I had to phone Auntie to come to the house, which she did immediately. She was strong enough to oppose his bullying. It would have helped to have been able to look into the future and see that years and years later, after two more wives, he would sometimes return to Mother – ostensibly because she made the best steak-and-kidney pudding. The two would sit by the fire having a quiet siesta, with Father relaxed and no longer having to pretend to be younger than he was, no longer having to be dynamic. He could tell her about his gall-bladder operation, his constant catarrh, his deafness and get some sympathy, which he did not really deserve.

But as things were in 1931, he drove her into a nervous breakdown. With the help of a woman doctor who had been at St Elphins, Aunt Richmal found a health-farm nursing home near Hereford, where Mother was sent for two months. All I could glean in the way of information was that her "system" was being drained and replaced with carrot juice.

Father also went away, which left us under the fairly relaxed supervision of Richmal and Clara, often conducted by phone, although we still attended frequent lunches and teas at The Glebe. Our two-month summer holiday was spent in glorious

Tommy neat and tidy for tea with Clara

freedom in the Plaistow Lane house, living independently of Dorothy, who was in charge of the child, then aged two. The daily cleaner agreed to cook for us, if bribed sufficiently, so we held dinner parties for our friends. For once we had enough cash.

We were back at school when our unfortunate mother returned, determined to divorce Father. She did not tell him this, when he also returned to the house. Instead she and Aunt Richmal had preliminary talks with a solicitor. Richmal's first consideration was to secure a home for us, so that Father could never turn us "onto the street" at a whim. He could easily give notice to the Plaistow Lane landlord (for houses were usually rented in those days) and then depart on one of his trips abroad. As a family we were very vulnerable.

Aunt Richmal found us a suitable house in Cumberland Road, just off Westmoreland Road, where new houses were being built. Father was indeed finding the upkeep of the large house more than he wanted to pay and a temptingly lower rent for a four-bedroomed house, paid to Richmal, was a good proposition. He did not perceive the ultimate intention. I had always assumed that the deeds had been transferred to my mother right at the start and it was not until I cleared and sold the house after Tommy's death that I found Richmal had withheld the transfer for twenty years before signing it across to my mother, when there was no risk of Father's wangling it from her.

While Mother was steeling herself to take the fateful plunge – for divorce was a very serious matter in those days – there were obvious marital tensions which were a great strain for the entire household, except for the baby. Father was travelling during the week and returning at weekends. When he left again on the Monday we all relaxed but within a few days we began to dread the next weekend. A spare bed was kept in my room for Mother to move into at any time; often she did so in the middle of the night. She had it all to herself in the term time.

The Dishers: Mother, me (16), Tommy (18) and Richmal Junior.
Note that gloves are worn in the garden!

Eventually, in 1934, she announced her intention of divorcing him and he was asked to leave the house. He sent a van to remove his furniture but we managed to buy replacements at local sales. Later he paid me a visit at Cheltenham and said, "Try to persuade your mother not to divorce me." But little did he know how strongly I felt; indeed, I was one of the prime movers behind it, alongside Aunt Richmal and Clara. I was at school when the decree absolute came through, following the nisi, but I had made Mother a smart Divorce Dress and chosen her hat for the necessary appearance in the High Court, where she was accompanied and comforted by Aunt Richmal, who wrote me a full account of the proceedings, adding, "Your Divorce Dress looked marvellous but I'm sorry to say I only noticed afterwards, too late, that her slip was showing." I should have been there.

Although Tommy had a different view of his schooldays, I was happy enough, being fully occupied all day, with plenty of friends and lots of action. For a while I belonged to an anti-Guide group, making fun of the Girl Guides among us who had secret signs and call signals, and held special meetings behind closed doors, which was all too earnest for me and like-minded friends. We were quite content, however, to light camp fires and brew up tea in billycans (add a blade or two of grass – it improves the flavour) in sheltered hollows of the nearby Cotswold hills when on group excursions. We visited places of local interest – Cheddar Gorge, stately homes and castles, Stratford-on-Avon and all the nearby cathedrals.

Another girl, whose 88-year-old uncle lived in the town, got permission for the two of us to pay him a lunchtime visit one half term. From a lifetime's habit he gave us what he thought was sherry before the meal and too late realised it was whisky. We then had white wine with the fish and red wine with the meat course. He was very hospitable. Neither of us had ever drunk anything alcoholic before and we were distinctly unsteady on leaving him. We decided to walk to regain our equilibrium and took deep breaths of fresh air to reduce the smell of drink, testing each other's breath from time to time. It was about two hours before we dare go back to St Austin's. That was my initiation, and it was with the same friend in the holidays that I started – and very soon gave up –

smoking a pipe.

A Swiss friend had a portable gramophone so we made parents and relatives bring us the latest popular records. Some had to be played quietly in the dormitory at dead of night, the sound muffled by eiderdowns. I improved my French from some Marlene Dietrich songs and managed a fair imitation of her deep husky voice. "Allez. Lêve-toi. Va t'en. Mon lit n'est pas trop grand pour moi." No doubt we acquired a French accent overlaid with Marlene's German intonation.

Young ladies off duty

Young ladies even more off duty!

Unfortunately Tommy had left Cheltenham by the time the two schools were allowed to hold a joint dance. During the spring of 1935 we were thrilled by the announcement that the top forms of each school were to attend a dance at the boys' college after the exams were over in the summer term. These dances would in future be held every year, alternating the venue from one college to the other. Our dresses would have to be inspected to ensure respectability. By then I had a boyfriend in Bromley and attended plenty of dances in the holidays, so selected my most demure style to take back to school. Although the front was cut quite high, the small vee at the back was considered too daring, so I had to fill it in with pink net.

For sheer novelty I enjoyed the dance more than most. It came straight from another century. Although we were all aged about 18 – some slightly younger, some older – our "houseladies", as they were then called, escorted us as chaperones. We were shown into the boys' largest hall which had a roughened floor that had been unsuccessfully processed to make it more slippery, ending up almost sticky. We stood at one end, clutching our little programme cards with small pencils dangling; the boys stood at the other end in a crowd, also clutching little cards. At some signal the boys were unleashed and bore down on us, starting to book dances with the girls they fancied. The rule was – no more than two dances with any one boy. Our chaperones circled round, inspecting the cards and trying to help the less popular girls. The boy I remember best was rather like Billy Bunter. He held me extremely closely, breathed heavily down my neck and his hot fingers roamed up and down my back. I made an inspired guess and asked if he was musical. Yes, he replied, he played the cello. Meanwhile the chaperones sat along the sides, watching for foul play. It seems incredible that this was 1935.

Afterwards, comparing notes, we decided that very few of the boys could really dance. We were not brilliant ourselves, for at that time we were not taught the social graces as were our friends at Westonbirt, another girls' school not far away. *We* had to work: our school's success was judged by the number of university places gained, the scholarships and the eventual degrees achieved. I managed to get Higher Certificate in pure and applied mathematics and physics (just the subjects that are scarce today) for at that time Cheltenham usually had good results in science. There were no grants in those days for further education and because of the divorce of my parents I was anxious to be independent. I could not have endured a financially straitened university stint, always wondering if Father would provide the next lot of cash. As it turned out, I had a financially straitened career instead.

Aunt Richmal had been more than surprised to hear of the Cheltenham dance. Before then not much that I recounted had been fundamentally different from St Elphins, except for the mixture of nationalities at Cheltenham and the rather liberal church arrangements. Naturally our uniforms were shorter and not so constrained as hers had been, especially for gym and games – hockey in the autumn, lacrosse in the spring and swimming, tennis and cricket in the summer term. She wanted to know all the school customs and had questioned Tommy the same way. My description, for example, of the antics we had to perform at the swimming baths to gain a bronze Life Saving Medal in my last term was reflected in at least one William story. When I reread the books I can find many part-plots and backgrounds that came straight from our schooldays.

In his teens, Tommy became infatuated with a number of girls but often had to worship from afar because he could not think how to get on friendly terms. His rather clumsy overtures were often brushed aside, so he developed a technique of following a girl home to find where she lived. He thought nothing of venturing up to the house and peering through the windows, hoping to get a sighting. One girl attended a local convent school in the Sundridge Park area and on dark winter evenings he would wander round the convent grounds, lurking in bushes until he saw her emerge. He always hoped to find an excuse, an opportunity of starting a conversation; but she never even dropped her handkerchief like a Victorian maiden, and there were no villains from whom he could rescue her. So he enlisted the help of an older boy, with me as junior back-up, to take more positive steps. We actually went up the path of her house and knocked on the front door.

It was opened by the girl's older brother, who was puzzled by our request to see Mr. Cresswell – a fictitious name we had chosen at random. We said we were due to play bridge with him at eight o'clock and had been given this address. The brother called out to his sister: "Joan, is there a Mr Cresswell anywhere in the road?" She came to the door, to Tommy's joy. No, she knew no one of that name but thought it might be the new people in the house nearly opposite. With profuse thanks we went across the road. They were still watching us from the open door, so we had to continue the act. Fortunately they closed it before the finale took place.

Only a second after our knock, a gruff and sinister voice came from behind the door: "What's the password?" I shrieked "Crooks!" and fled across two or three flowerbeds, closely followed by the other two. At a safe distance we conferred on this new and dangerous turn of events, deciding that the police must be informed. I still remember the deadpan faces at the police station as they heard our story and took notes. They thanked us for our service to the public and we went away certain of the next day's newspaper headlines: GANG OF CROOKS DISCOVERED IN KENT TOWN or perhaps POLICE ARREST CROOKS AFTER TIP-OFF. But there was nothing – not even a small paragraph.

We found out weeks later that the gang of crooks was in fact a father searching for his pipe in his coat pocket at the hallstand beside the door who, on hearing our knock, thought his son had forgotten his keys and so tried the joke that misfired. What an anti-climax! Only William could have understood our disappointment. The only consolation was Tommy's introduction to the beautiful girl; at least he now knew that her name was Joan. He used the end of the story to start a conversation the next time he saw her, but still without much success. It was several years later that a friend of mine from Bromley High School days married the brother Jack, and several decades later I found that a business associate of mine was by then Joan's second husband. Both Joan and Jack remembered Mr. Cresswell's bridge party.

Every time I saw Aunt Richmal, which was frequently in the normal way, she would ask "What have you been doing this week?" and she genuinely wanted to know. There was a great warmth about her and we could be sure of a sympathetic hearing even when the arrows of outrageous fortune that struck us were entirely our own fault. Her sense of humour was always ready to surface. She loved ridiculous situations and people, and noticed every detail of odd behaviour. "Don't look now but the woman at the next table is putting the left-over chocolate biscuits into her pocket. They are going to crumble as soon as she moves and the chocolate will melt and merge into the lining. She's probably got a dog at home who's given her a list of what he wants. I do hope she doesn't live too far away . . ." would be a typical café observation. Or if the service were slow she would describe some horrific imaginary crisis going on in the kitchen, behind the scenes.

She would have loved the current spate of "yer nos" scattered through broadcast interviews with teenagers and the like, also the pompous clichés from jumped-up adults such as "at this moment in time" and "so be it". Obviously William would have picked up some of these expressions, and used them in all the wrong situations. He would have taken "at the end of the day" quite literally, breaking all the rules and straining every sinew just to get some job completed before darkness fell. "The bottom line" might also have provided scope for misunderstandings. And I am certain that William would have saved every penny to buy a Political Football.

Richmal was a "good sort", as we used to say in our teens. She attended many school functions, usually escorting Clara and Mother and generally taking her place like the family father. When I was working she came to various functions where I needed her presence. We never asked for speeches but she would hold animated conversations with other VIPs and say all the right things, batting ably for whatever side we were on. We could count on her doing the right thing, although sometimes in an unconventional way.

Pre-war suburban life in Bromley, and village life in Bromley Common, was enlivened for us by Richmal's literary successes because each was celebrated by a family outing to London, generally to see a new musical show. Although Richmal, Clara and Jack favoured Gilbert and Sullivan shows, we did not. I, at any rate, was unashamedly bewitched by Ivor Novello's romantic operettas, which Tommy considered soppy; although having heard that a dramatic shipwreck was staged in "Crest of the Wave" he agreed to join us. He secretly enjoyed larger-than-life stage effects in other shows, and pantomimes were universally popular with all of us. I was known to love the funny men, especially those dressed up as women, like the Dames. Tommy used to study every movement of the jugglers and acrobats, which my mother viewed with considerable apprehension, for she knew what would follow when we got home. Above all I loved the comics who smashed dozens of plates with complete abandon and upset buckets of whitewash over floors, tables and chairs. How I longed to do the same! As for Tommy, he did these things anyway – though on a smaller scale – given half a chance.

Richmal went to many serious plays, especially historical dramas. This love of theatre was a continuation of the Cromptons' and Lamburns' passion for amateur theatricals in Bury. Within the family circle during her childhood, plays were written and acted at regular intervals. The greatest fun was dressing up, with the clothes and the props made by members of the family who were good with their hands. There was no wireless or TV so they made their own entertainment. Amateur theatricals are an important feature of the early William books and William himself is forever

Fancy dress made by Mother

dressing up. He manages to "borrow" many of the outfits he wants from his older brother Robert, who appears to have a very extensive wardrobe, frequently supplemented by his friends' clothes which include elaborate fancy-dress costumes.

Fancy-dress parties took place regularly in William's village and occasionally William was made to wear some outfit he hated, such as the knave in a pack of cards; an indignity suffered also by Tommy, when he was about six or seven. In a posed photograph he looks quite happy, resplendent in the outfit painstakingly made by our mother; but I remember his loudly voiced disgust at being made to look so foolish compared with his real tough self.

From the moment the new baby was born, my mother was usually too busy to notice what Tommy and I were doing. Satisfied that I was under strict control in the term time she failed to observe in the holidays my very high heels, plucked eyebrows, bright lipstick and the occasional false eyelashes, which in those days had to be applied with glue, one by one to the natural hairs. It was a lengthy job. "Margaret, whatever are you doing up there? Breakfast is nearly cold," failed to get results. "Coming Mother," I would say, but I could hardly appear with one Garbo-like eye and the other not finished.

Another secret occupation was the alteration of all my school uniform, to improve the fit. The school staff could never understand why I looked different from the other girls. They studied the outfitter's labels, which I left intact as proof of authenticity. My hat was one or two inches shallower than the others; it never occurred to anyone that I had cut the crown and brim apart, removed a section from the crown and put the two together again. If they had looked under the headband ribbon, all would have been revealed.

The writers on each side of the family had their advantages. As dramatic critic of the *Daily Mail*, Uncle Maurice Disher had to attend the first night of nearly every show and as a teenager I was thrilled to go with him from time to time. He introduced me to exciting people like Anna May Wong, Madeleine Carroll and even the designer of the R.101 airship, which crashed a week later, so the tragedy made a special impression on me. He also took me to circuses and introduced me to the performers behind the scenes.

Maurice seemed to know so many people, having worked

on several different newspapers as film or drama critic, also as columnist. At that time he was advising the BBC on their *Old-Time Music Hall* and circus programmes. A contemporary of Hannen Swaffer and James Agate, he was intrigued to find I had taken Agate's flat three months after his death, many years later – in 1948. It was a huge rambling place at the top of Shaftesbury Avenue from which Agate had written several of his Ego volumes. As it was much too large for me I shared it with several other people, but it was a changing population during the eleven years I held the lease. Alan Melville was in the flat above all this time but we never even said "Good-day."

In the 1920s and 1930s wherever Uncle Maurice went, all eyes would turn to look at him. He used to wear a dramatic black hat (almost compulsory for theatre critics) and had a pronounced limp owing to a childhood illness; he had to use a stick for walking, so we had a lame author on each side of the family. Maurice was married to a talented artist – Eve Disher – but they lived in separate flats, visiting each other from time to time. As recently as 1987, when she was 92, Eve's paintings were given a special exhibition for four weeks at Foyles Art Gallery in Charing Cross Road. She was described as "the last of the Bloomsbury Set", who had shared a house with the Stracheys. But sometime after the war Maurice found himself a delightful second Eve and they lived happily ever after, the last years of his life in Spain.

As children we were not really aware of the individual magazines and journals in which Aunt Richmal's short stories were being published, and only read them in the William books as they came out. Mother was always given a copy straight away and sometimes Tommy and I had copies of our own. When *William – The Gangster* was published in 1934, I was very excited to find the book dedicated to me – Richmal had kept it a secret. I had already received one dedication, in *William in Trouble* in 1927: "To Margaret (aged 9)". The very first had been to Tommy (*William Again* 1923) and the second to Mother (*William – The Fourth* 1924).

Later – in my mid-teens – I started to read Richmal's other books, the novels which were often family sagas with involved relationships and emotional dramas. I found to my surprise that I loved these books almost as much as the William stories and admired Richmal's analysis of character. Frequently I wondered how she could have such an understanding of romantic love when she had never been in love herself – not that this point was ever discussed within the family. However, she saw enough of every emotion going on all round her. I wish now I had asked her more direct questions but at that time we took the books and her fame rather for granted. We were, of course, delighted for her sake when she was asked to speak at functions and was interviewed for the press or radio.

It was on November 18th 1938, just after her 48th birthday, that Aunt Richmal received the first *Just-William* film offer, the fee being £1,000 from which she gave me £5. By January 1939 Fred Emney had been cast as Mr. Brown, which we all thought quite wrong, but it took the BBC much longer to find William. It was not until mid-February that Dick Lupino was selected to play the part.

I had a very kind letter from William that month, after complaining within the family about a shortage of interesting

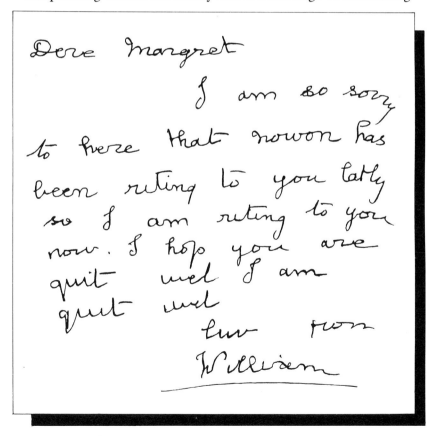

February 1939: William writes to me on Aunt Richmal's writing-paper.

letters. "Dere Margret" he began in very shaky writing, "I am so sorry to here that nowon has been riting to you latly so I am riting you now. I hop you are quit well I am quit well luv from William." There was no address or date. The three halfpenny stamps on the envelope were, of course, stuck on sideways. Someone should have told that boy not to insult the King. He had ritten on the same mid-blue riting paper and enveloap that Auntie often used . . .

Richmal decided to hold a celebration cocktail party in London and asked me to act as co-hostess, helping to receive the guests – all the people she had met during radio interviews and stage productions, also Mr. and Mrs. John Watt, her agent and his wife, many personal friends and several branches of the family. The ones I remember best were Leon Davey, a well known scenery designer who later married Gracie Fields' secretary, the actor Ireland Wood who was well known to our family, Richmal's old college friend Elsie Wilmore and another family friend of long standing, Stanley Rowland. Our cousins the Wrigleys, the Lamburn family and the Dishers all stayed on for dinner at the Kensington Park Mansions, a type of hotel where the party had been held. Early in March, several press reports on Richmal and the William film started to appear, the first

Garden view of The Glebe. Richmal's bedroom (central two windows)
was directly above her study

142

being in *Film Weekly*, then the second in the *Sunday Referee*. Clara had attended the party as an honoured guest, but it was to be her last party.

Donna Clara died in May 1939 aged 77, after only a few days' illness. She was taken ill on Wednesday May 17th and by the next day it was known that she had a clot in an artery and would be at least six weeks in bed. The next week would be critical, so the specialist arranged for day and night nursing. On the Friday Mother was all day at The Glebe, coming home very late. The next day they phoned for her to return at once but Clara died before she got there. Jack came to The Glebe and stayed two weeks with Richmal. Meanwhile I had 'flu so could not attend the cremation, for which I was thankful. For me Clara had been special and I could not have borne it.

Donna Clara, ageing gracefully, in The Glebe garden

X

Going to Work and War

In 1985 I saw an old lady crossing the road using my mother's system. With great courage she stepped fearlessly into the street regardless of the traffic, expecting it to stop instantly. It always did, with loud screeching of brakes. I watched her with growing apprehension, sometimes trying to steer her towards one or other of the zebra crossings whenever I happened to see her. She was new to our High Street village in the heart of London and was living in sheltered accommodation round the corner from me. I had been carrying her shopping and helping with her laundry for several weeks before I realised she had been Tommy's first boss.

Eveline Mary Ward, one of the early career women in the City, worked for an investment company where she became a reasonable expert on gold, having been sent to South Africa for six months to help with a report on two gold mines. At the age of 92, when I met her, she could still draw diagrams of the gold seams and the mining methods. She was mentally alert, had a great sense of humour and loved to talk about travel, having been to a great many interesting places. As her knees had lost their spring she walked slowly, bent almost double over a stick; but still saw herself as tall, strong and athletic. Once she looked up at me and said, "You're nearly as tall as I am."

At first I gave my name as Margaret. After knowing her for a week or two I wrote my full name, address and phone number on a piece of paper and said, "Any time you need me . . ." She looked at the paper. "Disher? We had a boy in our office called Disher." At the time I dismissed the thought. After all, there must have been other Dishers around. But after reflection overnight, I questioned her further. "What year was that – when you had that boy in your office? What was the name of your company?" When she said Central Mining & Investment Corporation, I knew for a certainty. The year 1934 removed any further doubts. "Surely it had an oil subsidiary in Trinidad?" I asked. She was amazed that I knew. Yet this was all I *had* known about Tommy's first job. He had managed to last three months before he was sacked – as I understood it, for being late for work each morning.

Eveline Ward had a different story. "He was useless at paperwork – absolutely useless. That's why I told my director the boy really had to go." "Poor little boy" I said. "It was his first job. He was only 18. You probably frightened him into a state of mental paralysis." She could be very fierce, even at 92. She terrified the waiters at cafés where we lunched on Saturdays, demanding the standards of silver service. When I challenged her with being unreasonable, she burst out laughing.

Probing further, I found that her job in 1934 had been to study all the newspapers and financial journals of the day and mark round any features or paragraphs she thought might interest the directors. She used to pass them to Tommy for cutting out and mounting. I could have told anyone what would happen. He would cut them out and then not know which was which or where they had come from. He would try matching up the typeset while everyone waited. Why was the boy taking so long? "Exactly!" she said. "But he did it time and time again. *And* he cut out the wrong features."

Poor Tommy! Much as I loved Eveline as she was in the 1980s, and found her far more entertaining than many friends of my own age, I could guess what she must have been like when in her prime, especially in a competitive financial sphere where women had to work hard and fight hard to hold their own in a man's world. It must have been a bad start for my brother's career because she was not the type to suffer fools, which was obviously her assessment of Tommy. How I wished he was still alive so I could go home and say, "You'll never guess what! I've met Eveline Ward of Central Mining." It would have been amusing to hear Tommy logic applied to the story and even better to let them meet. Unfortunately she will never read this account, for she died in 1988 after two months in hospital following a fall, when she broke her hip.

Tommy's dismissal caused worry and consternation at home. For Tommy himself it was a major calamity, shattering his dreams of gold and oil. Jobs were difficult in those days of economic recession; and he had neither qualifications nor references. I see now that he should have been a Physical Training instructor, perhaps at a boys' school, for the rugger teams he captained when older would have followed him to a man. In fact his main asset was team leadership.

Father was, of course, furious but in the absence of any other prospect took Tommy into the pickle factory – G. Sheldrake. As I was away in Cheltenham at the time I am not sure exactly how he came to fall into the barrel of brine, which made my father angrier still. Having been in the pickle factory once and seen the group of old women who sat peeling onions and laughing at visitors who started to cry on entering the shed, I can imagine the mirth that would have greeted Tommy's immersion. Mother had the impression that he had tried a balancing act that failed. The brine was normally used for preserving cauliflower, one of the factory's ingredients. He must have accepted a challenge, perhaps as an initiation ceremony, for he was not normally a show-off.

Alerted by the loud laughter, my father arrived to find his son dripping wet. It was far removed from his idea of suitable behaviour, especially in front of the workers. Father and son then had a flaming row, also in front of the workers. Tommy stalked out, dried himself and his clothes as best he could and made for the nearest Army Recruiting Office. By the time he got home that day he was, to all intents and purposes and barring the results of a medical, in the King's Army, Royal Fusiliers.

From September 1934 he was stationed at army barracks in Pembroke Docks until the early summer of 1935, when the Royal Fusiliers took over from the Scots Guards at the Tower of London for a seven-week duty. Now Tommy could come home on his days off and entertain us with stories about the ceremonies – the Spur Guard, the Wharf Guard, Main Guard and Challenging of the Keys ceremony, which was the best of them all. He even helped line the route at Tower Hill for King George V's Jubilee celebrations in May that year. Service at The Tower appealed to him far more than Pembroke Docks but his dislike of authority increased almost to breaking point; the regulation spit and polish required for his kit was ridiculous and he said so. Although always a man's man, he considered many of his fellow recruits to be criminal types. Probably their tendency to scrounge breached his code of honour.

We were always afraid Tommy would lose the keys of the Tower but in the end it was his rifle that disappeared. While on sentry duty he put it down and then was unable to find it

The Tower of London, once guarded by Tommy

again. Someone must have played a joke that misfired. As always, Tommy was the one to be set up, taking the blame. The Army took a serious view of the loss of a rifle and he could have been court-martialled. He returned with the others to Pembroke Docks on the scheduled date early in July, a few days before his 20th birthday, but at base they were there waiting for him. The sergeant major handed him his rifle and said, "You are on a charge. Leaving Government property in the Tower of London. Somehow I don't think you will ever make Sandhurst. If I were you I should try something else."

Tommy phoned Aunt Richmal, who already knew the rifle was missing. As a result she set in motion the purchase of his discharge, which cost £30, and he was able to come home. All this was around the time of the divorce, when I was totally preoccupied with swotting up maths and physics, trying not to fail Higher Certificate. Mother told me Tommy was having interviews and said she gathered that Aunt Richmal was taking advice from the local Westminster bank at Bromley. On arriving home from my last term at school, I found that he was due to start work early in August at the Westminster's Norwood branch, not far from the Crystal Palace, on a month's probation.

When the time was up we waited anxiously for news that his appointment had been confirmed but he was very casual about the whole thing. Eventually he admitted that his probation had been extended for another two months – information that sent a warning shock through Mother and me. "It's a last chance," we said. "Tommy, what *have* you done?" The next day Mother rushed up to the staff department at Lombard Street without his knowledge and there she learned what he had *not* done. Our worst fears were confirmed. It *was* a last chance. However, he survived, which was very important to us because there was no money coming in; Father was extracting his revenge for the divorce and continued to do so until the courts forced him to pay the alimony.

It was difficult all round. For my part I was disappointed and surprised to find the world was not waiting for me after all. It did not appear to want statics, dynamics, hydrostatics, calculus, trigonometry, electricity and all the rest. And I was hardly on speaking terms with my father. But I could sew. I took a job as a sewing hand at less than a pound a week and in the evenings and weekends made clothes for my mother, Clara, Aunt Richmal, also neighbours and friends. In that way I kept afloat before moving to Molyneux, where I made clothes for the Duchess of Kent (Marina), Princess Helen of Romania and stage star Gertrude Lawrence amongst other famous women of the day. It took ten more years for this experience to blend with the maths and physics, when I moved into production engineering in the USA. It is not possible to appreciate automation fully without knowing how difficult it is to do the work by hand.

Looking back through my diaries, I wonder how I had the time and energy to go to so many parties, mostly in London, where I lived for three months of those four years. I was then earning less than £2 a week, buying for my evening meal a pennyworth of chips and a herring for three ha'pence, which still had to be cooked. Aunt Richmal ordered the occasional food parcel from the Army & Navy to be sent to the impoverished refugee. I had only one plate, one knife, one fork and one spoon, so if friends came to dinner they had to bring their own eating implements. I had schoolfriends round me in the Bloomsbury area – medical students at the Royal Free Hospital – so I could go to their digs for a bath when I dare not risk the communal one in my own place. Then, having touched rock bottom and survived, I went back home.

As for Tommy, he did his best to like banking and even went enthusiastically to evening classes. One of his colleagues at another branch, who lived nearby and attended the same classes, often travelled on the same train in the evening and on one occasion at Bromley found Tommy still clutching all the bank's post which he should have put in a Norwood letter box. He would have taken the letters home absent-mindedly if he had not met this colleague, who happened to ask what was tucked under his arm. William, of course, had the same problem with letters in his charge.

At the Norwood branch another story concerned a customer who wished to inspect her deposit box. Before the time of her appointment the manager went to fetch it from the basement. Not having seen the light of day for a very long time, it was covered with dust so he told Tommy to put a duster over it before handing it to the customer. A short while later the manager saw him carrying the box through the branch with two new tea towels draped over it. When asked what he was doing, Tommy replied, "I couldn't find any clean dusters and thought the new towels would look better."

Everyone kept quiet about the William connection to avoid embarrassment at the bank. When Aunt Richmal was interviewed by a journalist from the *Sunday Referee* in March 1939 she told him the original prototype was her nephew, now aged 23, but asked that no mention should be made of his name because he worked for the Westminster Bank and was nervous of prejudicing his career. A photo of Tommy aged 10, looking quite neat and tidy in prep-school cap, was published but he was identified merely as "the nephew". Long afterwards I found that the bank staff had known all the time. There had been references in the local press.

Maurice Mason, a former Mayor of Bromley and now a councillor, used to live near our family and knew Tommy well. He repeats stories of Tommy's adventures out of affection for the "great character" that he was. He knows that Tommy was moved eventually from the Norwood branch to the Bullion department in Lombard Street because there were so many errors on his till. Tommy told him it had been decided he might do better dealing with money in bulk. But before that, the war was obviously on its way.

In the summer of 1936, less than a year after leaving the regular army, Tommy had joined the Territorials and was now in the Royal Corps of Signals. For many evenings the house vibrated with morse-code tappings; in the summer we pushed him into the garden to get some peace. He used to go on TA exercises and summer camps with great enthusiasm. It is still a mystery to me how, with rather clumsy fingers, he ever managed the technicalities of morse signals and field switchboards but he did, although he admitted to frequently "getting into a muddle". By the time war was declared in 1939, he was a lance corporal and was called up for full-time service several days before the actual war declaration.

Before he lost his stripe – Tommy in Royal Corps of Signals

Jack joins the RAF

He missed our move to The Glebe on September 2nd 1939 when we took all our possessions by Richmal's car, in several journeys. For days beforehand we had been filling sandbags with earth from The Glebe's garden and had already put up black-out curtains in every room. Soon after Chamberlain's announcement of war on the Sunday, September 3rd, there was an air raid warning; so we rushed into Aunt Richmal's study and sealed ourselves in with sticky gas-proof tape all round the edges of the door. The window was already sandbagged and sealed. As we sat there waiting for Armageddon it suddenly dawned on us that we had no food or drinking water. Fortunately it proved to be a false alarm and the All Clear sounded about ten minutes later. I gather this sort of resigned-to-death charade went on all over the Southeast of England that sunny autumn morning. It was the start of the Phoney War, which lasted until the following year, when war started in earnest.

Aunt Richmal had taken an ARP course, passing her exam in 1938 soon after the Munich Agreement, and I had attended First Aid lessons, becoming a VAD once war was declared. Auntie was called up for voluntary duty from 6.00 am to 2.00 pm on September 2nd, the day we moved our possessions to The Glebe. For a while she was on night shift at an ARP post at the boys' County School but managed to change over to daytime work at No.4 Report Centre in Hayes, near to The Glebe. Finally she settled into the Auxiliary Fire Service but much to her disappointment was not allowed to man a fire engine because of her "dead" leg, as she called it. She had fancied herself in a helmet but had to be content with telephone and tea-making duties.

Meanwhile I was attached to the Princess Plain First Aid Post in the Holy Trinity Church hall and occasionally had to get up in the middle of the night to cycle to the hall when the Alert sounded, which usually turned out to be a false alarm. Without any casualties it was all rather boring; the most active job I had was constantly refilling the hot-water bottle for the nurse-in-charge, because there was not much heating and she was cold.

By the end of October Aunt Richmal and I became rather brave and ventured up to London to have lunch and see friends. On her 49th birthday in November we lunched at her club in London, where we were joined by authoress-and-poetess Rose Fyleman, who had fairies at the bottom of her garden. By the beginning of December we were even more courageous, lunching at Genarro's in Soho, then going on to the musical "Under Your Hat". I had always longed to be a lady of leisure but now the luxury had arrived I became very restless. I had signed on the dole and was collecting 12/6d a week, but wanted a real job again. Then I found that the Meteorological Office *did* want maths and physics so I applied and was accepted early the next year, but soon afterwards declined the job and took another in the Aeronautical Inspection Directorate. During the next five years – after my department was transferred to the Ministry of Supply – this job was to take me careering all round the British Isles on slow-motion trains, on work almost entirely concerned with quality control, yet nothing to do with aircraft. I look back with astonishment at the enormous responsibility I had for my tender age, passing judgement on deficiencies in the execution of government contracts, one stage before arbitration. I knew at the time it was the finest job I would ever have.

At home, an Anderson air-raid shelter had been installed in a large hole dug in The Glebe's garden and covered with earth and greenery. When the real war started and London was being blitzed, Aunt Richmal, Mother and my young sister usually went into the shelter. I went in once but thereafter decided I would rather stay in the house and take my chance. Bromley Common had already been in the direct path of the Battle of Britain but now the heavy bombing was not so close, being nearer the built-up areas of London and the suburbs – which was the same all over the country. At this time I had occasional work commitments in London in the evenings while visiting the South, and usually took a taxi all the way home to The Glebe. On one or two journeys an air raid started while we were on our way and I still marvel at the courage of the taxi drivers who blithely drove on. It was like a film, with bombs dropping to the left and the right, setting buildings on fire, and we viewed the scene as if it had nothing to do with us, except for the occasional comment. "That was a near one." The truth was that we could only drive on; there was nowhere else to go.

One night I had to offer the taxi driver some hospitality when it was really too hot for him to return to London immediately. The family was in the garden shelter so I gave him something to eat, with some of my grandmother's home-made wine from stocks that fortunately lasted for several years after her death. When the All Clear sounded the family came in from the shelter, not at all surprised to find me holding a dinner party. At other times I "slept" in Selfridges basement, which had been turned into a vast dormitory for the public. People made beds of cushions and rugs but it was difficult to sleep. Bright young things played accordions and mouth organs and old men shuffled round spitting at frequent intervals. All through the night people laughed and talked in loud voices. Unknown to me, Eveline Ward was around, being an officious warden.

By 1943 Mother wanted to return to her own house in Bromley and as Jack and his family seemed likely to need our slot at The Glebe, we moved once again – unfortunately to be home for the first night of the V1 rockets which were immediately over Bromley. We stayed up all that night, fully dressed. A flickering flame from the engine showed up in the dark sky, then the engine cut out and seconds later came a huge explosion. This was something new. By the dawn we realised they were too small and too frequent to be suicide pilots in small planes, which had been our first thought, and by daylight we had assessed the weapon. If the engine was still making a noise as it passed over the house we were safe, at any rate from that one, and prayed it landed on spare ground. It was the silence between the cut-out and the crash that was so unnerving. Like ourselves, most of the neighbours were hanging out of the windows, watching. Yet when I reached London the next morning, no one knew what I was talking about. Censorship had prevented any mention on the radio or in newspapers in case it gave the Germans valuable information on the accuracy of their new weapon. They were left guessing for a few days whether the rockets, later nicknamed Doodlebugs, had arrived or dropped into the sea. Hastily I stopped talking, for we were always being reminded that walls had ears. I took the lurid story back to my base in the Midlands, where I had to return that day, and so was not in London when the more powerful V2 rockets arrived a few months later. Fortunately the family escaped that hazard unharmed.

Tommy's war was slow to start up. During the Phoney War

he managed to play golf more often than we thought possible for a member of His Majesty's armed services, coming home on leave very frequently. In fact he was back at The Glebe within a week. According to my 1939 diaries, he turned up every few days. There is no record of how far he had travelled. He generally came back to play golf and get me to press his uniform, which did not appeal to his superior officers. Eventually we put all the golf clubs on a train and sent them to his unit, at his request. I think by then he was at Catterick in Yorkshire and the journey home wasted too much valuable golf-playing time. He was rather upset when he was unable to take his clubs with him to Africa.

Proud owner of plus fours: Tommy aged 18

When Tommy lost his lance-corporal's stripe and was promoted to private during the first few months of the war, he explained to us how he had entered into physical combat with a sergeant, during a dispute over who had got to the bathroom first: another crime for which he could have been court martialled, but fortunately was not. He lost pay several times for various "incidents" but we never knew any of his army colleagues, so were unable to get a first-hand account of his wartime adventures.

Tommy on leave – with Richmal Junior, Mother and Aunt Richmal

His love life was as complex as one might expect. At the start of the war he had become formally engaged to a girl of 16 who was still at school – the headmistress thought the ring was "very nice". That does not seem so extraordinary now but at the time it was generally considered unsuitable and something of a joke. It did not last and the girl returned the ring in the time-honoured way. There were other romantic friendships which proceeded towards a ring but were braked – I believe by him – when they turned too serious. Despite his pursuit of romance, he seemed determined to protect his bachelorhood.

There is little doubt that soon after Tommy reached North Africa in 1942 Rommel started to retreat, so word must have got around. Although we were always amused by Tommy, just below the surface lay a permanent anxiety about what he was likely to do next and this was obviously intensified during the war years. Aunt Richmal followed every facet of his career as if he were her own son. Yet neither she nor my mother kept a record of his army days – which were described in graphic detail, censors permitting, in his letters from the age of 24 to nearly 31. My mother kept these letters for a long time but eventually they disappeared, possibly destroyed by Tommy himself. One friend who had read them said they were unique.

His spelling was, of course, his own invention; he had never seen any harm in deviating from the norm. There was no law that obliged him to keep to a specified system. Yet the curious spelling tended to detract from the drama of his despatches from the front, as with "Role on death", which he wrote to me. I remember that at one stage of his desert experiences he scrounged an extra mug of water, which was always in short supply, and managed to drink some, clean his teeth, wash his hair and all the rest of him. We never knew in what sequence, so debated with Aunt Richmal the possibilities. He was always fussy about his teeth so they would be sure to come first, but we were not so sure about his hair. We decided body next after teeth, with hair last, in the same water – which by then would be almost half sand.

Army records show that his overseas service came under the heading "Middle East" until June 1945. His medals included the Africa Star with 8th Army Clasp and the Italy Star, in addition to two other war medals and the Territorial Army Efficiency Medal. So it appears that the Italian campaign, after his African service, was considered to be Middle Eastern. I am not sure how my Italian friends would

Brew-up in the dessert

react to this information. At any rate, he was in the battle of El Alamein, the invasion of Sicily and the Salerno landings, which took place in September 1943. He stayed with the fighting there until the summer of 1945, after the armistice in Italy, and was not demobbed until February 1946. He remained in the Royal Army Reserve and even served again in the Territorial Army Royal Signals from March 1950 to the end of 1951 and was not released from all Reserve Liability until 1959. But he became "browned off" with army life, although his wartime and postwar colleagues were much more congenial than the prewar regular army men.

I was told that on his return from the Middle East, Tommy never talked much about the details of war or the exact Italian route taken by the 8th Army. He was so glad the war was over and anxious to get back to civilian life that, like most of his contemporaries, he threw himself into his work at the bank, again at the Norwood branch. Although Army records gave the demob date for 6458258 Signalman Thomas Edward Lamburn Disher as February 27th 1946, Westminster Bank archives show February 17th as the date he returned to Norwood, so it looks as if he returned to work even before his demob leave expired. I was in the USA at the time, having left England in November 1945 and not returning until June 1946, which was the first time I caught up with Tommy since Christmas 1941.

When I questioned him on the Desert Rats' living conditions in Africa, the terrain and his reaction to real war shoot-ups, he gave me fascinating descriptions of the vast barren expanses of sand and stones, of huge sandstorms and bitterly cold nights. The men cut each other's hair, washed their own smalls – very occasionally – and went in for a surprising amount of PT and athletics while waiting for action, which pleased him. Playing football, they kicked up more sand than anything else.

He described the awe-inspiring sight of Sherman tanks roaring in formation across the desert. The shelling and gunfire lighting up the darkness at night was frightening yet wildly exciting; in contrast he found the infantry's resort to bayoneting, on both sides, degrading in terms of modern warfare, although it had been essential in the circumstances. Even long after the fighting was over he still seemed constrained by wartime censorship, unwilling to give details

1990s haircut for Tommy in wartime – far right

of the El Alamein campaign. I had the impression that he found it rather confusing, even in retrospect. He never wanted to return in peactime, even to Italy, as many ex-servicemen have done. Yet there is no doubt that he had been glad to fight in North Africa and Italy, having been stirred to fury by Italy's brutal invasion of Abyssinia in 1935, and was ready to get to grips with the aggressors even if his only weapons were field switchboards and radios.

Tommy – the Tommy

158

XI

The Merchant Adventurer

My father announced that his death had taken place in Nebraska in the autumn of 1923 when he drove into a river and his car overturned, pinning him underneath. I had always understood that he had given a lift to a tramp, who had struggled out and gone for help; but the tramp hero was sometimes excluded from the story. Father survived after artificial respiration but for the rest of his life he claimed to have died in the river. After a month in hospital he continued his journey by rail to San Francisco where he caught a boat for Tahiti, not returning until the spring.

Wintering in the sunshine was to be the pattern of his life for another seven years. In between these visits he made his way to exotic places, conducting tours to many parts of India, Burma, Kuala Lumpur, Penang, Singapore, Hong Kong, Shanghai, seven Japanese cities, Honolulu and the same transAmerican route we had taken to cross en famille from San Francisco to Montreal, but with more reliable transport.

Sometimes he turned up unexpectedly at our small Bromley house when we thought he was thousands of miles away. On one occasion I went rigid with fear, watching a door open very, very slowly, fraction by fraction – obviously not moved by a cat or the wind. His face then appeared round the edge as a "funny" surprise, which left me trembling and shivering for several hours afterwards, having to be wrapped in blankets and calmed down. It is possible he was trying to find out whether Mother was alone during his absence – but there was no one else except Tommy and me.

It was about six years later that the family crisis came. He had been travelling during the weekdays with his secretary, and returning to us at weekends. There was some evidence that she had put money into his business and was demanding its return. He wanted to take cover behind family commitments but it coincided with our wish to be free. It was a bitter divorce and his reaction was to cut off all financial support for my mother and young Richmal, by then five years old. I was still at school, while Tommy was just starting his first job. It was not until after the decree absolute in 1935 that alimony of £4 a week was awarded to my mother, a very small sum by which to support herself and a child. By his curious system of accounting it appeared that he earned only £12 a week and standard alimony was set at one third. It was the old, old story – all the travelling was, in effect, on the business.

He had a legal right to see "the child" every few months; so on occasional Saturdays, as I had left school by then, I had to act as intermediary, meeting him and delivering her for the afternoon. The time came, to my relief, when she was old enough to go on her own, although once or twice Mother had to answer the door and exchange a civil greeting. Then, eight years after the divorce, she decided to meet "the other woman". She suggested that Father should bring her to tea. He accepted instantly.

So the two women met in those wartime years when food and domestic commodities were scarce. Freda brought a gift of suet and Mother offered her jam for the son, born in 1936. They were both surprised by each other. Freda found Mother younger and more vivacious than she had expected; and Mother found Freda quite different from the stereotyped image of a husband's mistress, being more like a staid governess.

By this time my father was very deaf, even at the age of 56, and was not aware of what the two wives were actually saying to each other in deliberately low voices. According to my mother he sat with an inane smile on his face, concluding that they were getting along quite well. "Unfortunately he doesn't understand children," said Freda. Mother agreed, quoting many examples of his unsympathetic treatment of Tommy and me. Freda found that he grudged their child quite small things, which cost almost nothing, like a nightlight to reduce fear of the dark. They continued comparing impressions and experiences while my father, who had no idea that they were exchanging criticisms of his character, smiled to himself at his diplomatic skill in getting them together; they seemed to be getting on so well, conversing on "women's subjects".

In this way the second wife became our liaison officer. She persuaded my father to give Mother a car, which – when it finally arrived after months of promises – turned out to be a curious amalgamation of two which had suffered rather severe crashes, put together by one of his mechanics. Female members of the family also received diamond rings, for what reason I am not sure. He had probably bought a gross at some liquidation sale.

The car was a great joy to my mother. She had learned to drive when in France and proved to be a good driver by all accounts. Although she had really wanted a Renault, she had to be content with this mongrel. It was principally a Standard, with many alien parts and panels. The engine came off its springs every now and then so she kept a spade beside her in order to heave it back again, a sight which tended to startle passers-by. She was well known in Bromley, sailing along – as Aunt Richmal said – like Harry Tate, a music-hall comedian of that time who had a funny car. Mother's was black when delivered but she painted it maroon. She never understood what made the car move and when told that her battery was flat, she asked what shape it should have been. She also made local history by driving for two miles with a completely flat burst tyre, complaining that something was wrong with the steering. This was the car on which Tommy learned to drive.

In the mid 1930s, about the time of the divorce, my father felt the urge to enter politics. Through his European travels and extensive contacts he had become convinced that there would soon be another war, yet the Labour Party was using Disarmament as its main election platform – and no party seemed to realise the seriousness of Germany's intensive rearmament. At his own expense Father had earlier distributed 30,000 copies of a four-page leaflet warning Camberwell electors to ask all candidates whether they supported the necessary British defence measures in view of the political conditions in Europe. This was dismissed as "alarmist" but led to his contesting the North Camberwell constituency as an Independent in the 1935 General Election. He came in last of three candidates, with a Pacifist winning.

He then became president of the Camberwell branch of the Labour National Party, serving also on the National Executive, but to his disappointment was not selected as a prospective candidate for the wartime Coalition Government. Later, in 1944, he fought a by-election supporting Churchill, but lost. Then the North Camberwell branch asked him to stand again in the 1945 General Election but as he was known to be a factory-owner he did not go down well in that area, which solidly supported the main Labour Party under Attlee. At least he had the satisfaction (for he was definitely an egoist) of seeing his face on the posters up and down the Old Kent Road: "Labour National – Vote for Churchill – Vote for Rhodes Disher as your local MP". He claimed to have polled as many votes as the Conservative candidate but the Labour Party easily exceeded the two put together. This was, however, the one time he managed to keep his deposit –

progress indeed. Although we laughed a lot in the family, it is only fair to credit him with courage; because stones, mud and bricks were thrown at his car and he endured a lot of mockery in the local press. His campaign had included several far-sighted reforms, including amendment of the divorce laws. Many years later this came about.

One of the most ironic incidents about that time must have been the baptism of Freda's son at the age of 14. Being a convinced atheist, Father had refused to allow the usual christening and baptism of the boy when a baby; yet on reaching his teens he became impressed by Christianity and the Church's teaching. His schooling at Dulwich, then

Wellington, included religious studies which made him realise he was not a member of the Church. By secret arrangement his mother and mine – the two wives – accompanied the boy to be baptised. My father never knew that they had conspired to arrange this repudiation of his wishes.

Although they had lived in London all through the war years, this second division of the Disher family left England for South America in 1948. They had travelled extensively in Europe during 1946 and 1947, reviving the tours, but not much further afield until Father made an exploratory journey through most of the South and Central American countries and decided that Uruguay was in the best position to serve as a suitable headquarters for import and distribution of the various products made by his British factories.

In the event they stayed only two years and during that time he succeeded in increasing his UK exports, particularly the curry products. Amongst the countries he visited was British Honduras, now called Belize since independence, where he arranged to buy an 8,000-acre estate, to grow pineapples, maize, beans and mahogany. At that stage he abandoned Montevideo and returned temporarily to England, again travelling in Europe, including Vienna where he bought wood for his London sawmill. There his Austrian courier – the one I had fancied when I was only five – was responsible for introducing him to Luise.

When Freda realised that prospective wife No.3 was on the scene, she was outraged and phoned my mother for sympathy. "Gwen, he wants me to meet her. As if I would meet such a woman!" And when the divorce seemed imminent, she said, "I hope it won't be reported in the local paper." "Ours was indeed reported," replied my mother. "They get lists from the Courts of forthcoming divorce hearings, so you can't keep it quiet." "How dreadful," said Freda. "So all the neighbours will know." She never stopped to consider who was at the receiving end of these confidences. For our part we were all rather pleased. One divorce might have been construed by some people as my mother's fault, but two divorces? Obviously it was Father.

Aunt Richmal thought the new scenario was hilarious and for my part I returned home more frequently to catch up with the latest developments, much amused by the turn of events.

Our spy inside the Disher empire, one of Father's managers, alerted us at about the same time as Freda's distraught phone call, so I probed to find out more. All one could discover was that prospective wife No.3 was Austrian, about my age, and that she was already in England with her brother and his wife, who were also going out to Belize with my father. The brother was apparently a good engineer and would be a great asset for the estate my father had bought, or so he explained. Eventually, when out in Belize, he quarrelled with this new brother-in-law, just as he had done with Freda's brother many years before, at that time going as far as a court case to prove which of them owned a leather armchair.

However, at this stage the in-law-to-be relationship was still idyllic and they looked forward to an interesting new life. Our spy reported that all three Austrians would be at the annual dinner dance of one of my father's companies, a printing works, and that Freda would also be there without knowing of Luise's presence. This situation was something we really had to see and although normally we had little or no interest in his companies' activities, now we announced our intention of going, en masse, as the first division. This made our spy very nervous indeed; I think he was afraid there'd be a punch-up. I assured him he need not worry – our contingent would be the soul of discretion and tact.

The family was relying on me to locate the Austrians. During the dinner I failed to find anyone out of the ordinary, different from the firm's employees. It was a matter of looking for three strangers, together in a group, who would probably have no friends to greet or talk to. There was no help from my mole. I was suddenly afraid that we would never find them and the whole evening would be a disaster.

When everyone else had gone through to the dance floor, I cornered the mole. "You are going to be cut into tiny pieces," I said, "unless . . ." At that point my father came up to us and said, "Margaret, I wonder if you would like to meet some Austrians who are going out with me to British Honduras. The man is an excellent engineer. He will be accompanied by his wife and sister." I gave the mole a withering look while I smiled at my father. "Yes, that would be interesting," I replied. They were falling into my lap.

They were tucked away at a small table at the far side of the dance floor, completely inconspicuous. Freda was at the high table with her son, then 16, and my mother. As soon as my family saw me sitting with three people, they realised I had located the target. First my mother came over and Luise flushed up as I introduced her. When ten minutes later Tommy and my sister headed for the table, it was obviously getting dangerous. In true gangster style, I muttered out of the side of my mouth "Not too many of us at a time" and returned to the high table. Father sat there wearing his self-satisfied smile. At a safe distance from Freda I told him, "Nice people. They'll be useful."

That night Luise, at a hotel with my father, could not sleep. Something was bothering her. Finally she said, "Tom, they knew about us. I am certain." He said this was impossible but the next morning phoned Mother to tell her of Luise's suspicion and asked her outright. Knowing she must not betray the mole – or Freda's original phone call – she answered "Yes, Tom, I know a certain smile on your face. I could see from the way you were looking at her." Immediately he wanted advice on the alimony for Freda. What did food cost per week? Unknown to Freda, my mother prepared a budget for her needs, much more generous than her own had been; a new flat and a car were provided as well as a substantial income. So all was settled amicably and Luise went on her way to that torturous climate and ramshackle "house" on a remote jungle estate, miles from anywhere.

As doyenne of the three wives, Mother eventually received a state visit from Luise's Austrian Mamma. "You vill look after my lil gel, ja?" So Mother agreed to see, as far as she could, that no harm came to the lil gel; who was at that time nearly 40 anyway, with one previous marriage to her credit. Now she had embarked on a doubly hazardous adventure, comprising my father *and* the jungle, which apparently grew twice as fast as they could cut it back. In comparison, Freda had had an easy time and even Mother's Tahitian adventure seemed luxurious.

Aunt Richmal enjoyed every detail of the story. In her time she had paid a lot of money for theatre tickets but here was a larger-than-life family drama on her own doorstep, being unfolded stage by stage. At the same time, on a more serious level, it proved she had been correct in her early assessment of her brother-in-law. She had viewed his amorous and business enterprises with a mixture of distaste and mistrust.

Now at a safe distance, she was the first to see the humour of the situation and much relieved that she need never see him again. She was amazed, in view of the comparatively large income allocated to Freda, that my mother had not been offered or asked for more than the £12 a week to which Father had promoted her. It may be that Freda had invested capital in one of his companies and he felt obliged to pay her interest.

Father would not give up his dream of a colony, so tried to encourage others to join his British Honduras expedition. He had issued a statement before leaving England which described his aims:

"I have bought, as a start, a factory on a few acres in the city of Belize, and over 8,000 acres of timbered land with sea, river and road frontages. So far I have spent only a few thousand pounds in clearing and planting pineapples, bananas, maize, rice, beans and peas, but I am now in England for several weeks, buying heavy-powered equipment for economical clearing, cultivation, saw-milling, electricity generation and insect extermination with the aim of converting in a few years many tens of thousands of acres of jungle into an estate producing each year, not only much valuable timber, but a wide variety of foodstuffs to reduce imports and increase exports. No doubt I shall have a somewhat lonely life for the first year or two, but not too lonely, as I have over one thousand records of delightful classical music and get weekly periodicals to supplement my large library. In a few years I hope to have at the sea-shore, houses equipped with electricity and running water, gardens beautiful with fruit and flowers, boating, swimming and fishing facilities to attract visitors who, finding life cheap, warm and healthy, may decide to make their homes permanently with me.

There is an abundance of fish, lobsters, prawns, turtles, breadfruit, sweet potatoes, yams, rice, maize, beans, peas, tomatoes, lettuce, avocados, pineapples, oranges, grapefruit, mangoes and bananas. As I intend raising cattle, sheep, pigs, turkeys, ducks, geese and chickens – meat and poultry, milk, butter, cheese and eggs should be plentiful and cheap."

But his dream went completely adrift owing to lack of research into local conditions and the total mismanagement by a local "expert" appointed to organise the project during Father's absence in Europe. The middle of the jungle was cleared instead of the edges, which meant that houses and wells had to be built and transport provided for villagers working on the estate. It was my father's opinion that 100 acres could have been planted within 500 yards of the existing road. As it was, unnecessary time and money had to be spent clearing and constructing new roads into the plantation. It was also cleared at the wrong time of year – something no one had thought to mention – it should have been done before he bought the land, or left for another year. Although the "expert" was the main customer, with a canning factory in Belize City, as soon as he saw the results of his mismanagement he demanded a salary in addition to the 10% commission arranged.

There was also the problem of labour's attitude: anyone with capital was automatically considered an enemy. The "expert" paid 25 cents per quart for planting, based on instructions for three seeds in each hole 18 inches apart; but being almost unsupervised the men put large amounts into a few holes, then went to sleep for several hours. Large quantities of corn and beans were planted, with no arrangements for shelling. There was pilfering on a grand scale and criminal misaccounting, with no receipts, and many personal expenses charged by the expert to the business. He hired a car for every small journey.

A management report had claimed "We have over 75 acres of planted pineapples in excellent condition" but Father found only an expensive wilderness. The first year's fruit crop, estimated by the expert at $20,000 in value (in the early 1950s) proved to be worth less than $100. He was, in fact, being taken for a ride. So he scrapped the pineapples and planted coconuts and bananas along the lanes already cut into the estate. Then more than fifty of his mahogany trees were cut down "by mistake" and the logs sold off very cheaply to local contacts.

The jungle itself caused immense difficulties involving heavy maintenance costs. The two four-wheel drive trucks often became stuck in the mud and had to be towed. People found it difficult to walk in the deep mud, although Father preferred walking to the violent jerking and shaking of the trucks. For a while he camped in the middle of the estate in very primitive conditions.

Poor Luise! When they returned to England she told us that their house, which was on the road to Belize City, had been built to my father's specification with the upper half of the rooms open but filled in with a plastic mesh to ventilate the house yet keep out mosquitoes and larger insects, with the lower three feet of wall made of wood. But he forgot about the tropical rain. It came through the open half, driving through the two-storied house in torrents caused by the strong winds and hurricanes which frequently blew up in the area – a much greater danger than in Tahiti or Montevideo. And the roof was not exactly secure; although made of corrugated galvanised metal, it came adrift quite frequently. The high humidity also upset Luise, just as it has angered the British troops stationed there since independence. They have demanded some air conditioning.

Because of the lack of facilities Luise insisted on going to New Orleans, the nearest point of real civilisation, for the birth of her son Douglas, in 1953. Although she was the youngest of the three wives – young enough to be Father's daughter – jungle existence and my father's character eventually disturbed her mental balance. Father had given Mother a nervous breakdown years before but Luise's condition was more serious and she had to be taken from Belize to a psychiatric hospital in Kingston, Jamaica. After her recovery we heard she had suffered similar problems caused by the Russian advance into Austria during the war, before she met my father. Possibly that was what Luise's mother had been trying to tell my mother. So it had not necessarily been a good idea to pension off the older wife, Freda, and replace her with a younger version.

My father finally managed to create his dream on a miniature scale but with heavy financial loss all round. He surrounded the strange house with orchids and other exotic plants and flowering shrubs. Most of the animals, fruit and vegetables he had planned to farm were lodged in the grounds, but on a much smaller scale. He built another four houses for his technical staff, with electric light and running water. There was also a granary, storehouses and a shop. Presumably Luise's brother and his wife lived in one of them before they parted company from Father – for reasons unknown to me.

His final throw was to grow castor oilseeds but then the price suddenly dropped when China started selling huge crops at 15% below the world price. This was almost a repetition of his experience in Tahiti, when the price of vanilla had dropped in twelve months from £1 to one shilling a pound. In the end he gave up, cut his losses and came home. As none of his businesses would willingly let him through their doors, he bought a barometer–manufacturing company in London's Clerkenwell area and was very happy going to work every day, driven by Luise, until the age of 86 when he had a stroke and died soon afterwards in hospital, two years after Aunt Richmal's death. Over the years Father had amused, amazed, angered and frightened us. But I have to admit he had enterprise; even William's imaginary explorers could hardly equal his sense of adventure.

XII

Shotgun of the Bullion Van

William and Tommy were both rough and tough characters, keen on action. Both needed a gang of supporters ready to obey commands. They also needed a certain amount of danger, which they were driven to create if none already existed. So it seems fortunate, on reflection, that almost by accident Tommy found a dangerous and responsible job not normally listed under boys' careers for the late 1940s. Forty years later the work would cause no surprise, but at the time we found it difficult to explain to friends just what he did. Aunt Richmal had a better idea than the rest of us because she questioned him more closely; but once again we had a nagging worry, for he became secretive, intimating that he handled the nation's wealth. After his death I had to search out former colleagues to trace his career following his demob in 1946.

Back in the bank, Tommy was soon moved from the Norwood branch to the Bullion department at the Lombard Street headquarters. According to Maurice Mason, Tommy knew that his failure in the banking exams would have blocked his route to promotion within the branch. Despite that drawback he considered himself fortunate to have a job, for in the mid-1930s, when he was taken onto the permanent staff, it was extremely difficult to get work anywhere. And all through the war he was secure in the knowledge he could return to the bank.

When new faces turned up to work at the Bullion Centre, the old hands would say: "What have you done? Who did you offend?" as if it were a prison. Yet once installed – however much new entrants grumbled – the department held a fascination for them which they could hardly bear to relinquish. It seemed to me there was a special camaraderie between these three-cornered pegs who could not be fitted into the bank's round or square holes. Most were unconventional characters, some more so than others.

Tommy was a natural gang leader and, probably as a result of his athletic strength, he was given charge of one of the Westminster's bullion vans that delivered cash from

Lombard Street to the branches. For the first time he was in his element. Just as William would have dreamed of having several million pounds on board an armoured truck, Tommy had found an adventurous job that became even more exciting when bandits started hi-jacking companies' wage vans. Although no attacks were made on the Westminster bullion vans, I believe he was secretly hoping for a fight.

The clerk in charge, known as the Custodian, had to stay on board throughout the journey. Tommy told the crew what to take out and deliver according to his list for each branch. "They were a difficult team," one of his colleagues told me. "On one journey, halted at traffic lights beside the ruins of a wartime bombed-out branch, the messengers pretended they had arrived at the next delivery point and asked what to take out. Tommy looked at his list and said, 'Go on, man, ten bags of half crowns.' The messenger seized the chance to make some drama. 'But the branch has been burned out,' he exclaimed. 'It can't be,' said Tommy. 'It's here on my list.' But there it was – a blackened shambles. Tommy still insisted the cash should be delivered, at the same time cursing bureaucratic muddle. Most of the crew knew that the rebuilt branch was only round the corner and by the time the lights changed and the van drove on, a lot of aggro had taken place." It was said that the messengers were jealous of the clerks but apparently Tommy managed them very well and even took his gang home for tea when the van was delivering nearby, much to Mother's surprise.

I remember her accounts of these visits, when she had no advance warning to prepare a suitable tea for six or seven men standing unexpectedly on the doorstep. Often they had pub lunches in the countryside, providing – of course – they had finished their rounds and the van was empty. But there are many reports of the crews' really disgraceful behaviour and their frequent attempts to rile Tommy, all taken in good humour. Perhaps his youthful experience with the rough types in the prewar regular Army served him in good stead.

I tried to discover the built-in security system but he would never tell me, merely indicating that new protections were being added almost daily. It was all highly confidential, which he enjoyed. You can imagine William with great important banking secrets entrusted to him . . . Tommy would protect them with his life if need be – providing he could still get home early to play golf. In the summer it was light enough and the van finished earlier than the offices, much to the annoyance of other clerks.

One story about the Shotgun of the Bullion Van, as Tommy became known, recounts how the van broke down in a side street shortly after leaving the Bank of England on its way back to the Bullion Centre, which had by then been moved away from the City area. As at that time they had no radios, Tommy went into a café to phone for a mechanic's help and while they waited the whole crew disembarked. They were happily drinking cups of coffee in the café when the police turned up, desperately searching for the van. Tommy had given the wrong street name by mistake and mechanics had failed to find them. A general alert had been put out to find and rescue the van and crew, thought to have been kidnapped. I could not discover whether the van had been full of cash or empty.

Another unfortunate breakdown was when the van-door lock disintegrated in the middle of a run and they had to find a way of securing the doors for the rest of the journey. Tommy sent one of the crew to buy some string in a village shop and they tied the handles as best they could, untying and retying at every delivery. Unfortunately when driving up a hill the knots gave way, the doors burst open and bags of coins littered the road. The crew hastily rounded up the scattered bullion, retied the string and proceeded on their way.

Tommy's most famous delivery was undoubtedly one to the Bank of England. Bank procedure laid down that on this trip two clerks had to be in charge of the cash plus the messengers and the driver. With Tommy and colleague John Taylor in charge they were approaching Threadneedle Street when two of the messengers started to fight and accidentally set off an alarm. As the van arrived at the Bank of England the gates closed instantly and barred their way. The alarm had done its job. With the noise still deafening the area, Tommy told the driver to carry on, round and round "The Old Lady" while they wrestled with the switches, trying to turn them off, all staff now subdued and rather anxious. By the fourth or fifth tour round the block, and with much waving of arms and shouting, Tommy and John made themselves understood. "It was only an accident. For goodness sake open the gates." Or rather, that is a polite version of what was said.

As he remarked later, it was nothing to do with him. He was just unlucky that his team chose to fight at that particular moment. "He was very accident-prone," said Norman Shapton, his chief at the Bullion Centre. "It was never his fault. Well, not always." All Tommy's colleagues made allowances for his eccentric character and behaviour. "We understood him," said Shapton. "In fact all my predecessors as managers had nurse-maided him, so I continued the tradition. Because he had back trouble and bronchial problems and so on, we let him turn up later than the others every morning because he thought a daily morning swim would cure him. I seem to remember there was a doctor's certificate."

He worked on a very short fuse, according to one colleague: "He used his physical strength to get his own way, even on station platforms when travelling home. He could be sure of a seat in a train carriage unless he had to give way to the opposite sex, which he always did." They noticed he was careful to keep himself in good condition and I remembered his PT exercises every morning on and across the kitchen table, which eventually made it very wobbly. Apparently he often kept a bottle of milk in the van and one lunchtime went into a pub with the others, asked for a glass, sat at a table and poured out the milk while the others had beer. The landlord saw what he was doing, went mad and told him to go.

John Taylor, who remained a friend for the rest of Tommy's life, explained how my brother came to be parted from the van he loved. After the merger between the Westminster Bank and the National Provincial Bank in 1969, it was decided that cash deliveries were to be contracted out to security companies and so the van teams were no longer needed. This really upset Tommy. Having found an exciting job that got him out and about, with shorter hours, he felt that to have this cut from under his feet was a monstrous betrayal of all he had worked for. He asked for early retirement and was refused.

After the bank vans were stopped there came the time when Tommy felt he could no longer load or unload the outside security vans. It was because of the fumes in the van depot, which at that time was an enclosed area and by Tommy's standards was poisonous and too hot, sometimes reaching 85°F. There were often as many as twelve vans at a time delivering, many of them keeping their engines running while the cash was unloaded and taken through to the Counting House. Those were the days before people were aware of the dangers of pollution.

So Tommy joined the staff doing the counting, where a high productivity was important. Today cash is counted by machine but at that time the manual counting was not always reliable and Tommy had to keep putting in his own money, £10 at a time, to make the total correct. That enraged other clerks who spent hours trying to find why they had £10 too much, and Tommy would have great difficulty in proving that the surplus belonged to him. When the clerks were counting cash it was usually under "dual control" and in this way each man was, in effect, watched by another. But Tommy sometimes got left out and during a VIP's visit he explained the system: "Sam's watching Joe, Frank's watching Doug, Jim's watching Bill and Heaven Alone knows who's watching me." This did not go down quite as well as he expected.

During the 18 years that Tommy did the bullion run, he became well known in the branches. According to Maurice Mason, they instituted their own local adjustment service to reconcile wrong deliveries after the van had left, because Tommy had so many ways of confusing them when taking away the surplus cash and delivering new bullion. Yet another report from a retired colleague throws a different light on the subject for apparently, on the first day the Bank undertook collection from a major retail chainstore, as a brand new service, a mountain of cash descended on the Bullion Centre. When it had been counted, no one knew what to do next. Tommy stepped forward and, in his colleague's words, "by some incredible feat of home-made bookkeeping managed to get things sorted out, in this way saving the day". This is exactly how William, apparently a champion bungler, could at the last minute rescue a situation from disaster – if he put his mind to the problem. The same colleague confirms the difficulty of Tommy's £10 till "shorts and overs" but explains that he could not be bothered to find the source of an error or declare a difference, which suggests intellectual laziness rather than stupidity. Personally I always bore in mind his ability at bridge and chess. Otherwise it was easy to underestimate him, to your cost.

However, the Bullion Centre decided to manage without Tommy's accounting methods and he was moved to Credit Information, which he hated, although in the few weeks he was there before early retirement was finally agreed – at a much reduced pension – he made some more good friends. He still missed his Bullion comrades.

"He would never have made a real banker, but we understood him," repeated Norman Shapton. "He had to have an adventure a day and that could not be done in Credit Information." He had worked with Tommy for 23 years and been his manager for six, so he knew him well. "His eccentric character was definitely that of William and we all knew that, although he denied it." In so many ways Tommy had liked the Bullion Centre, where his leg was pulled mercilessly, particularly about his being a bachelor. Shapton had a serious talk with him, saying he should get married. "We even produced suitable candidates from nearby offices. He was a handsome chap and some of the girls seemed quite keen. But he would not even take them out. He preferred to find his own." There was a strong rumour that he was fond of a girl in the Bank of England but it came to nothing. He continued to the end a bachelor.

Although Tommy was a good team man, Shapton observed strange sides to his character. He was often alone, and he usually had a book with him if he sat in a pub at lunchtime. If people spoke to him he would talk easily but he never drew attention to himself, as some do in pubs. He was not a big drinker, either. One might have expected him to have grown into a complete extrovert, but that was not his style. I knew the books he would have been reading – all the great and famous novels I had devoured as a schoolgirl. Like William, Tommy had scorned books in his youth and so only discovered them later in life, when some of his aggressive energy had burned itself out. It took a long time to do so.

This energy had full scope in the bank's sporting activities and even today at the Norbury Club various incidents of his career are recounted by retired members, often with much amusement. Golf and rugger stories predominate. Ivor˙ Waters, who captained the Bank's "B" rugger team for a number of years in the late 1940s and early 1950s, was always amused by Tommy's rugger outfit, which consisted of Army issue for quite a long while, with khaki socks and baggy khaki

Tommy (seated, right) in Westminster Bank's 'B' rugger team,
captained by Ivor Waters

drill 8th Army shorts well down to the knees but at least topped by the official Westminster sports shirt. Tommy usually challenged the referee's decisions and wanted long discussions on infringements; not necessarily on his own account, but as a matter of Rugby principle. He was very popular with the younger players and for a while captained the "C" rugger team. But his unconventional methods upset the Sports Club establishment and he was moved upwards again to the more senior "B" team.

Maurice Mason played rugger with Tommy before and after the war; both of them continued to play into their fifties. Remembering rugger incidents, Maurice told me: "He was as tough as old boots. He never seemed to feel pain and went on playing with blood streaming down his face." He described a match against hospital medical students when Tommy dislocated most of his fingers. The students, seeing the chance of some professional practice, clustered round and between them held him down and pulled his fingers, which at least made Tommy wince. Once the problem was resolved and several pieces of sticking plaster had been added to his face, the captain said, "Follow the normal procedure. Give him the ball, point him in the right direction and give him a kick up the backside. He is sure to score."

Another "B" team member, who sometimes went away with Tommy for inexpensive golfing weekends at a country hotel in Sussex in the late 1940s, described his golf as good but slow, deliberate and ponderous. "He was a good chap to have as a friend," he kept repeating when I saw him later in Leeds. All his bank colleagues seem to have known that he was William, although they confirm my impression that Tommy himself never said a word on the subject.

Tommy captains Westminster Bank's 'C' team.

177

The rugger and golf crowd describe his graduation in postwar years from bicycle to motor bike and then to car, which must have been my mother's Standard mongrel. He used to borrow that until it collapsed, after which he bought his own Mini. In the 1940s not many of his contemporaries in the bank had a car, so he was useful; especially for away games when they all had to work until lunchtime on Saturdays, then travel and change into sports gear.

One Saturday, soon after he had started to drive, he offered to take three of them to Shortlands, a few miles further into the green belt, for a round of golf. At the first hill on the road he admitted defeat, got out and offered the wheel to any of the other three who might know what to do. At the top of the hill he insisted on taking over again, cursing other cars and particularly the cyclists. "They always get in the way," he said as he drove onto the pavement and round a lamppost to avoid a cyclist. After stopping at traffic lights, he backed into a bus.

By then the two men in the back were cowering on the floor, and the front passenger hung on grimly as Tommy drove anticlockwise round a roundabout. He reached Shortlands Golf Club undamaged but in an effort to park the car he demolished a three-bar gate. The three friends staggered out in a state of shock, whereas Tommy was completely calm and proceeded to play "faultless golf, cool as a cucumber" according to two of the victims, Ivor Waters and Alan Goodrich, who laughed wildly at the memory forty years later. "At the end of the round he offered to drive us all back to the Sports Club. We preferred to return by train but found it difficult to explain why."

I never went with Tommy on golfing expeditions, considering one enthusiast in the family quite enough. He was a great stickler for golf etiquette and had long stories to recount which were invariably met by a glazed look on my face and Mother's. She would say automatically, "Did you, dear?" every time he paused for breath, following her initial cri de coeur: "Don't put your muddy shoes on the kitchen table!"

XIII

Tommy Carries On

The last six weeks of Tommy's banking career were spent in the very place where years before he had been a young soldier – for Natwest's Credit Information was in a red brick building overlooking the Tower of London. He felt a sense of bereavement after leaving his friends in Bullion, having worked with some of them for 25 out of his 37 years in the bank. His sadness was relieved to some extent by the kindness of his new colleagues, who did their best to initiate him into the mysteries of filing. Just as North Africa and Italy had been in the Middle East according to the Army, here in the Foreign Documentation department, Cyprus and Malta were in Africa. The filing was international, with some very complicated names and addresses; languages had never been his strong point and now his idea of geography was also proving to be different from the bank's.

Finally, on December 27th 1973, he joined his old mates at Bullion for a farewell drink, when they wished him luck. Only John Taylor, 20 years his junior, was to remain a close friend; they took holidays together for the next ten years.

The family had always looked forward to Tommy's holidays throughout his working life. On his return we gathered round – Aunt Richmal the keenest – to hear what had happened, for something always did. Most of the time he was puzzled about the way we questioned him closely, finding his stories so funny. "What was your hotel room like?" asked Auntie on one occasion. "Oh, it was OK except that I couldn't sit out on the balcony" replied Tommy, causing us to imagine dangerous structural defects or nudist neighbours. "Why not?" asked Auntie. He seemed to think we were just stupid. "There wasn't one," he replied shortly.

We wanted to know if he had made some new friends on his latest holiday. "Yes, one or two. One woman was quite friendly at first but then turned very cold and formal." We made him recount every word he had said, eventually arriving at the root of the problem. Following an after-dinner coffee he had remarked – very politely, he assured us – "If you will excuse me now, I will go and join the younger set in the bar."

He denied that she had any right to be annoyed. "She was obviously *not* one of the younger set. She couldn't *possibly* imagine that she was. Anyway, she would not have liked the noise they were making so there was no point in asking her to come too." The Tommy logic once again. We tried to explain that people do not see themselves as they really are; they keep to the memory of how they used to be.

Tommy did all the classic things such as losing his luggage and leaving his passport behind when travelling on a package tour to Austria, and having to return home to collect it, rejoining his group a day late. On the whole he was not really keen on foreign countries; the food was peculiar and foreigners usually spoke unintelligible languages. But he would put up with that in order to swim in a warm sea or lake, with a sunny sandy beach. He found the smaller villages in Majorca perfect and would start the day swimming at 6.00 am; and I have no doubt that subconsciously he was imagining Tahiti's beautiful lagoon.

As he grew older I insisted on inspecting his holiday clothes several weeks in advance and was usually appalled. "When do you plan to wear *that*?" I would ask about shorts that had grown too small for him or shirts that had seen many better days. He used to argue passionately because he loved them as old friends and failed to see that he had put on weight and that they were nearly worn out anyway. He was genuinely not bothered about what people thought but on the other hand I was anxious he should not become a joke, the object of giggles and whispers. There was no one to explain that he was William. So I went shopping, for which at his age he was pathetically grateful.

But his clothes were always odd. As I have noticed with other men, the very worst are saved "for gardening" and this embraces the entire weekend even when no gardening is done. Some of Tommy's cardigans were simply holes sewn together. Trousers were wide and baggy, with the crutch approaching the knees, left over from some unknown period in the past.

In retirement Tommy became a man of set habits. It was nothing as precise as shoes in a certain place, because his possessions were rarely to be found in the same place twice. But he liked to have a set routine for playing bridge, shopping, playing golf, swimming and holidays just as he had

John Taylor in 1989

done when working. For golf sessions he often linked up with John Taylor, who rarely knew until the last minute when he would be free so that the planning and replanning was somewhat complex and frustrating.

John was no longer in the Bullion Centre and by now had found his real mission in life as the Sports Secretary in the bank's Support Services, with responsibility for organising matches, competitions and charity sports functions such as sponsored walks. From him we have a good description of their holidays together, sometimes on the South Coast but often at Bacton in Norfolk as paying guests of Mrs Burton, the wife of the local vicar.

At Mrs Burton's Tommy usually woke early, fetched a pot of tea from the kitchen and tuned in to Radio 3. Other visitors would find him still in pyjamas, blocking the landing leading to the only bathroom, sitting in the landing armchair with his legs spread out (the only comfortable chair in the place, he said) and drinking one cup of tea after another, absorbed in the early-morning concert. Women in their curlers en route to the bathroom must have disliked stepping over and round this strange man. Later the other visitors would look on with amazement as he ate a huge breakfast. According to Mrs Burton he usually worked his way through a whole loaf of brown bread before starting a large plateful of bacon, eggs, sausage, fried bread and mushrooms.

Mrs Burton is an excellent cook and taught him to make the brown bread he liked so much. Afterwards, back home, he often phoned her for emergency instructions at critical stages when something had gone wrong with the baking. He entered into lengthy correspondence with the McDougall's home economist who acted as breadmaking adviser. In fact he improved the recipe by adding honey, extra butter and other ingredients; yet eventually it became necessary to investigate what was giving me indigestion. His bread never rose, partly because he always insisted on roasting a chicken at the same time – something the experts said could not be done, since they both needed different temperatures. But he did it and every week gave me a loaf to take back to London. It was a long time before I realised that the indigestion lasted as long as the bread and if I stopped eating it the situation improved. Finally I discovered he was adding generous quantities of washing soda instead of bicarbonate and he was shocked when I said these crystals were normally used for cleaning greasy sinks and floors. He had used it regularly for cooking vegetables as well and whereas I have never really recovered from ten years of ingesting washing soda, he seemed immune.

Mrs Burton's guests were mollified and perfectly understanding once she had explained the identity of her strange guest who ate her superb meals with such gusto. The same explanation calmed another hotel on the seafront. Who was this man, said to be staying with her, who expected second helpings of every course? Just William. That explained everything; all was forgiven. They had thought him odd, sitting by himself studying everyone in the lunchroom as if he were the CID. Gradually the explanation spread, without his knowledge but possibly initiated by John. Tommy was completely unaware of the whispers or the fact that he was given VIP treatment.

The two of them usually went swimming at Mundesley nearby. The beach was normally crowded with children and parents in the school holidays. One time they changed on the

182

beach, as usual leaving their clothes beside a breakwater. When they emerged from the sea Tommy's clothes were missing. They searched the beach and finally saw a shirt sleeve emerging from the sand where some children were building a castle. In John's words, "Tommy went mad, shouting at the children and pulling his clothes out. He chased them but in turn was pursued by several mothers. He caught one boy and whacked him, whereupon the mothers set on Tommy. Fortunately the whole episode had been seen by an elderly woman who stood up for Tommy." Although there was no malice in his character, like William he stopped at nothing to get revenge when occasion demanded it. His bursts of anger were short-lived, however, and he could laugh more than William did. It is surprising how rarely William laughed. In the books he was really rather serious.

Other incidents on Norfolk holidays included a royal gaffe. Tommy and John decided to visit Sandringham House. Needless to say they got lost and wandered into the private apartments, followed by another group of visitors, and all walked happily onwards until they were confronted by a very angry official. Tommy never had a good sense of direction and rarely read instructions.

There were episodes of narrow escapes in the car, broken tree trunks just missing them, confrontation with other drivers and frequent breakdowns. An entire family called at the Bacton Vicarage to complain about Tommy's treatment of their young son when both cars became locked together in a narrow lane. The vicar calmed them down with cups of tea and diplomacy. John, who had escaped through a car window into a field of cows in order to rock the cars apart, bore witness to equal faults on both sides. There was very little damage anyway – it was more a matter of hurt pride.

For my part, I went to great lengths to avoid getting into his car. When visiting home, as I did most Sundays, I would stress my need for fresh air and exercise in walking to and from the station. Only torrential rain outweighed the danger of a lift. If he failed to see another car, he simply had not seen it – which he thought exonerated him from all blame. He had mental and physical tunnel vision on a lot of matters. My mother sometimes returned from long journeys with him, after visiting my sister in Norfolk, with bruises on her forehead until I rigged up an amateur seat belt in the car; for this was several years before the official belt-up. It seemed to me that a woman in her seventies should not have to go through that ordeal. I always hoped they would go by train instead.

It was when going on holiday sometime in his fifties that he was obliged to use the railway and thereby reached new heights of nonconformity. He had started out alone for Yorkshire but his car broke down and he was stunned to learn that the repair garage needed a week for the work involved. He had no alternative to packing up his possessions into cases and carrier bags and accepting a lift to Northampton, the nearest station. Having decided that his driving slacks were perhaps too scruffy, he changed his trousers whilst on the platform, waiting for the train.

Not understanding our amusement at this account, he explained that his roughly packed possessions – meant only for the car – could not be left on the platform if he changed in the gents. True, we agreed, they might be stolen. But on the other hand, he could not take the luggage into the gents because the floors were usually in a mess. True again. So he chose the only other possibility. And he was perfectly

On holiday in Norfolk

respectable. He had underpants. He was wearing a fairly long jacket. He was more covered up than most people on a beach. Why should anyone make a fuss? Again the Tommy logic defeated us. He really did not care what was "done" or "not done".

Despite Tommy's love of golf, he was suspended from his club from time to time. This was the Sundridge Park Club where he played quite a good game, with a handiap of 14, and won several cups in competitions. His longest period of suspension followed a fight, when he was in his sixties, with a fellow member of similar age. They were both naked at the time. They were separated and send back to their respective corners by the club steward. The fight had started after the other member had soaked Tommy's clothes when taking a shower. Tommy had emerged from his cubicle, dripping wet, to find his bundle of clothes in much the same state. Obviously the bounder deserved a good thrashing. The sight of two elderly naked men fighting was too much for other members, who fetched the steward before one or other contestant had a heart attack.

There were frequent bizarre episodes of stolen goods. It was not Tommy who did the stealing but others who stole from him, or so he thought. Once he had mastered the knack of reporting incidents to the police – which made a change from being chased by them – he reported stolen bicycles, stolen raincoats and stolen cars. He had left them in certain places and returned to find them missing. Even fellow members of the Bridge Club were suspect. He would give a long and detailed description to the police and then be uncertain what to say when he found the missing item still at home or parked in a different road from the one he thought. From all accounts, I gather Tommy was not alone in this type of misunderstanding.

He was once asked to leave the Bridge Club, at least for the rest of the day. Garlic was the problem, though not to Tommy – only to his family, friends and the Natwest Bank staff. Apart from the fact that he liked the taste, garlic was one of his health fads. He believed it would cure or ward off colds, coughs, indigestion, rheumatism and a long list of other potential hazards, though in reality I am not sure it did any of these things for Tommy. Bank friends said that he used to take his own sandwiches to work, stuffed with garlic.

Presumably the Bullion van reeked of garlic but on one occasion when he took his sandwiches into a public house and started eating, he was furious when the landlord asked him to leave. However, I had carefully trained him not to use garlic anywhere near the food he was cooking for me.

After his retirement, Tommy had gradually taken over the cooking and shopping at home. Realising that my mother could not carry on much longer with the housework I gave him a cookery book for beginners, with colourful pictures of mouth-watering food, in the hope of catching his interest. Although for most of his life food had simply been placed in front of him, he now discovered that producing it was quite a complicated business. He used to take Mother with him on shopping expeditions to West Wickham, Bromley or Beckenham and still went swimming every morning, sometimes taking her along to watch.

Once he began to take an interest in cooking, Tommy verged on being a health fanatic. He cooked dandelion leaves and told me, "They're good for you." I ate them obediently. They were a lot better than some of the vegetation he had

made me eat as a child. Now he had a passion for runny honey which tended to get rather out of control, spreading to door handles, light switches and banisters and collecting dust over a period of time. He was finally persuaded to change over to a more stable thick honey, fortunately not so fugitive.

His cooking was, on the whole, surprisingly good. He had standard meals each day of the week. Sunday it was roast chicken, largely in honour of my visit. Monday it was cold chicken, Tuesday chicken soup and sausages, Wednesday bacon and eggs, Thursday fish, Friday and Saturday something else, I forget what. If ever I suggested visiting the household on a different day of the week I was told this was not convenient because they were only having bacon and eggs. Personally I like bacon and eggs but he was shocked at the thought of domestic dislocation. There could never be any thought of changing the routine.

So I was not surprised when in 1977 the *Sunday Times* had difficulty in fixing an appointment for a photographer to take pictures of Just William at the age of 62, to coincide with a William TV series. Tommy refused to find any suitable time to see them. They had phoned, suggesting a day. "No," he said. "We go shopping on Tuesdays . . ." Well, what about Wednesday? "No, I do the laundry on Wednesday morning and play bridge in the afternoon." All right then, Thursday? "No, a nurse calls to check on my mother then." And so it went on. They were unable to make any appointment and got no pictures.

However, a few weeks later a double-page spread appeared in the *Sunday Times* supplement based on photographs supplied by my sister – several pictures of my aunt both as a child and grown up, with my mother and uncle and with my grandparents, also one of Tommy and myself as children. The only other picture of Tommy was as a schoolboy, looking abnormally tidy. Of course he had never liked being equated with William. He found it embarrassing and would rather not know.

By the 1970s Tommy had developed a protective paternal feeling towards a grandfather clock that had been in the family for many decades. It was temperamental to say the least, sometimes striking the wrong hour and other times staying silent when it should have struck. Tommy tinkered with the chains, weights and pulleys, which he did not understand, then started phoning friends. "I wonder whether you'd care to come over for a meal sometime soon. We haven't seen you for some time . . ." "No, not since the last time the clock went wrong. Has it gone off its rocker again?" Tommy would admit that it had and add, "Yes, please – do bring your tools." He had been overjoyed to find that a new neighbour was an amateur enthusiast and the entire road seemed to heave a sigh of relief.

The strange behaviour of girls had always puzzled and upset my brother. He would chase them until they responded, then take fright and retreat. One local girl went to see my mother and complained that Tommy had embarrassed her with family, friends and neighbours by letting her think she was on the verge of becoming engaged and then suddenly avoiding her and her entire family. She seemed to think this constituted a breach of promise – although she had to admit, there had been no promise. Presumably she thought my mother could fix things for her.

On finding the suitcase of photographs after he had died, I was unable to recognise more than five of the girls. Some were holiday photos, mostly taken in England. There was one of him with the schoolgirl fiancée at the start of the war and another with his first real love, Ruth Barlee, who was five years older than Tommy – a considerable age gap when he was only 18 – and who never took him seriously. A year or so before he died he met Ruth again, by then twice widowed; he had recently become friendly with her younger sister Molly and she had re-introduced them.

It had been a painful experience to realise that he was now regarded as old by younger women who had once responded to his advances. For years he had talked of women acquaintances being "on the shelf" without realising that the phrase also applied to him. But they could often catch his emotional nerve, even arouse a fierce jealousy, which would prompt him to charge around making accusations of faithlessness. Like many macho males, he had little understanding of finesse. I cannot imagine William having a delicate technique for courtship – devious, perhaps, but never subtle. Tommy's ability at chess and bridge was no help when it came to the inexplicable female psyche.

Having little regard for the "done" thing all his life, he was always at a disadvantage with women. He began to see that in courtship he should comply with the accepted idea of correct behaviour but was very unsure of himself. If he invited a girl to the theatre he bought a box of chocolates – and brought home what was left over. Why not? It would come in useful for the next time or for someone else. He was astounded when I told him the remainders should have been left with the girl. I should have been more watchful of his social graces: I had tried to train him. He was not at all mean – quite the opposite – and was upset when we judged such actions to be social blunders.

The subtleties of unspoken signals baffled him. He once sent jewellery, fortunately not expensive, to a woman he had met on holiday in the same way that anyone else would send a postcard, in effect to say, "Have arrived back safely. I was glad to have met you." In reply to my questioning he told me, "No, I didn't get particularly friendly with her. But I was glad to have a companion when swimming in the early morning. There were very few people up at that hour." I tried to explain that jewellery was inappropriate. It usually conveyed a message of personal admiration, of love, a romantic message. This news appalled him. That had not been his intention.

Going further, he invited himself to stay with another holiday acquaintance, a widow. She had a flat in a South Coast town. "You can't just park yourself on someone you hardly know without an invitation," I said. "Apart from anything else you'll embarrass her with the neighbours, who are sure to be nosey. She can, of course, say you are her cousin, but no one will believe her. More importantly you will give her the impression that you are personally interested, again romantically, which you are not. You just like the town she lives in and want to do some swimming." But he went anyway, not once but several times, with the inevitable result that she got hurt. "You keep sending the wrong messages," I told him.

"Say it with flowers" was advertised through all the florists' shops and Tommy thought this was a good idea. He'd got some nice ones in the garden. Having read that a single rose was romantic, he tried to advance his cause with a local girl but since the best roses were over he took a single chrysanthemum instead. Her mother opened the door and so he offered a marriage proposal with the flower, using the mother as intermediary. Having decided that marriage would, after all, be a good idea he called every day with a flower (today she tells me that he varied it sometimes with a cabbage) and repeated the proposal. He trusted that perseverance would bring its own reward but after a while found the procedure too traumatic. "You should have made sure she was interested in you first," was my sisterly advice. "Otherwise no amount of flowers and proposals will do any good." He was rather upset at being turned down so many times – it might be all right at 20 but not at 60.

William and Tommy could not understand girls

People thought that because he looked after his mother, Tommy had outgrown his interest in girls. Not so. Yet he had some narrow escapes. Quite late in his life two sisters appeared to set their sights on the house and devised a plan by which both would move in to live with Tommy and Mother. They assumed she would die sometime soon, then

Mother kept this photograph of Tommy by her bedside from 1935 until her death in 1981

one of the two should marry Tommy and at the same time see that the other sister was also secure. Whether they had drawn lots for his hand, I am not quite sure. After all, he was a fairly eligible bachelor with two pensions, some savings and had let slip that the house would be his. They were extremely annoyed with him when my mother turned down the essential first stage of the plan.

He enjoyed writing to girlfriends. Quite a number of romances flourished on paper despite his erratic spelling and writing, although I think he took endless trouble with these epistles, keeping a dictionary beside him. He looked up the words he knew he could not spell. It was the others that let him down. Once rather sadly he said to me, "It's funny how fond you can get of someone by letter and how well you can agree and understand each other but when you meet you're like strangers." Again my sisterly comment: "That's because you're both wearing your party manners in a letter. It may have been drafted out first, then amended and improved until it represented the image the writer wished to project, which may not have been really true. Letters are very deceptive. They are often a snare and a delusion."

None of us could anticipate his fits of obstinacy, which would surface at the most unexpected moments. My greatest embarrassment at his behaviour concerned an American I had located in Atlanta, Georgia, through studying the phone directory there. It is rare to find the name Disher anywhere at all but occasionally I still check on the phone books when abroad or in the UK. So it was very surprising to find a Thomas L. Disher in Atlanta. My brother was Thomas E.L. Disher. What a coincidence! I had to dash for my plane but at least had time to note the address; and after I wrote to let him know we had a duplicate Thomas Disher in our family, he came to my flat unexpectedly while passing though London. We were able to exchange information on relatives and ancestors. His family had always understood their roots were Dutch; we thought ours were Scottish, derived from Ditcher, the ditch-diggers, or else Dishart, like Barrie's Little Minister.

I said, "Let's phone my brother so that the two Thomas Dishers can speak to each other." He thought that a good idea and when Tommy's voice came through on the line he expected to take the receiver. But no. "Why should I want to speak to him?" asked Tommy. My optimism sank like a stone. "Well . . . you know I told you about him, living in Atlanta. I found his name in the phone book last year. It's such an extraordinary coincidence, being a rare name. And his mother's name is Margaret – stranger still." But nothing I could say would persuade him to speak to his namesake, sitting next to me there in London. I had to put the phone down. I did not know how to explain things to the American. After a lifetime of explaining Tommy to other people, I was at a loss. "That's just Tommy," was the reaction of people who knew him well. And I never asked him for an explanation because it *was* just Tommy. He may have resented an infringement of his persona. He may have been taken too much off guard, unable to think what to say. He could have been in the middle of some intricate job, resentful of the interruption and unwilling to switch his thoughts.

I remembered he had taken much the same attitude when some cousins from Australia turned up unexpectedly in London and wanted to visit Tommy and Mother. He would not agree. I was always the one left to explain it away. William was not quite so rude but he could be obstinate and often resented visits by cousins, uncles or friends of his family; mainly because they were grown-ups and usually got in the way of his own activities. It was another matter if William himself invited people into the house, when he expected his family to embrace everything from tramps and thieves to visiting artists – and of course the stray dog Jumble, who was rejected by the family several times over at first. William could be rude, too, as when he told a visiting schoolmistress, "Mind your own business."

The call of the Church, which was felt by both sides of the family, eventually reached Tommy. He must have been influenced by the family's religious faith, especially our mother's. She ran a local prayer group for sick people in the Shortlands parish of St. Mary's, visiting them and monitoring their progress, then typing a report for the circle of parishioners who prayed for them. This was before the days of photocopiers and her efforts with carbons were laborious; sometimes I helped with the typing on her rickety portable. Tommy became involved while still working for the bank; he often delivered the reports and sometimes checked on patients' progress. By the mid 1960s he was spending a lot of time reading the Bible and his bullion-van crew tried to make fun of him when they found out, but he took no notice.

Tommy wanted to be fully ordained into the Anglican Church but was persuaded instead to study for a lay readership. In 1968 he passed an exam for the first time in his life, and was afterwards licensed as a lay reader by the Bishop of Rochester. The Rev. Douglas Redman, vicar of St. Mary's (Shortlands), confirms Tommy's eagerness to be of service wherever he felt he could help. He conducted services in local homes for the elderly and in nursing homes, and there is plenty of evidence that these parishioners looked forward to his visits. He continued to check on people who were ill in their own homes. At the Church he assisted with the Sacraments and gave rather lengthy sermons when his turn came on the rota, which was always a time of great tension in our household. Aunt Richmal was delighted that her nephew and original protégé had taken this step, which happened less than a year before she died.

William preaching
to Jumble and Ginger

His Williamesque character mellowed a little but did not really change. He retained a remarkable ability to misunderstand a situation and the St. Mary's clergy were frequently nervous lest he miss the point of their instructions. On one occasion they managed to get him out of the Bishop's Throne only in the nick of time; he had thought it a rather comfortable chair. He was always very apologetic when such incidents occurred and – as always – allowances were made for his complex character, which was viewed with amusement and affection, tinged with frustration. They all knew he was eccentric and it was therefore impossible to know what he would do next. If he could face the wrong direction or unintentionally offend protocol he would do so, and be mortified afterwards. Usually he had the best of intentions yet he could be obstinate and inflexible, with a one-track mind when set on some specific course. He became incensed by injustice, on behalf of others, not so much for himself. "Tom was very chivalrous," the Rev. Mr Redman told me, "and very good at dealing with the ladies of the parish." I found myself wondering if they had auburn hair and blue eyes, which would have appealed to William.

When I questioned John Taylor about Tommy's activities away from home – off the leash, so to speak – he described him as very moral. For a lay reader at St. Mary's the least breath of scandal would have been unfortunate, so I was amazed when visiting home one Sunday during his absence on the golf course to be greeted by Mother's assertion: "Tommy's keeping a woman in his room. You must do something about it." I asked for the evidence. Had Mother seen the woman? Was he taking food up to the room? Had she heard a woman's voice? Had she heard her going to the bathroom, up or down the stairs, out of the front door? The answer to all these questions was "No." I said what an awful fate for the invisible woman to be imprisoned in the room, never going out, starved of food and water. A look of doubt began to appear on my mother's face. I said "If it is not correct, you must not say things like this. People may believe you and gossip round the parish, and as a lay reader it could do him harm." "But I saw a woman's nightdress on the bed," she replied. With that I went up to the room and opened the door. Of course it was empty, with no sign of female habitation. I looked into the other rooms. When Tommy came in from playing golf I said, "I hear you've got a woman in your room," and he burst out laughing because it had been Mother's own nightdress on the bed in her own room. He had been sorting out clean clothes for her and she had picked it up, saying, "Whose is this?"

Sadly that episode was the beginning of her becoming confused. We had no idea how to treat it and could not help laughing from time to time. She started to confuse Tommy with her unfaithful husband of so many years ago. She accused him of kidnapping her and keeping her in his house; she wanted to go home. I told her to pay up the ransom and she laughed. Once she turned to him and said "How's your mother?" It was impossible not to laugh, and she joined in.

Darby and Joan (Tommy and Mother) 1980
Where DID he get that shirt?

Most of the time she was rational and I was delighted that Tommy looked after her so tenderly and with so much patience. She became his child; their roles were now reversed. Always she wanted to knew where he was, even when he was only in the garden or the next room. He had opted out of having a wife and family but had now, finally, accepted responsibility for another human being. At first he had rebelled, for after a lifetime of freedom it was hard to accept the demanding role of carer. But there was a spiritual bond and understanding between them and possibly the very fact that he was, at long last, really needed by someone was his compensation and his raison d'être. He died only two years after Mother, so the return to freedom was short-lived, which I found very sad.

FAMILY TREE (2)

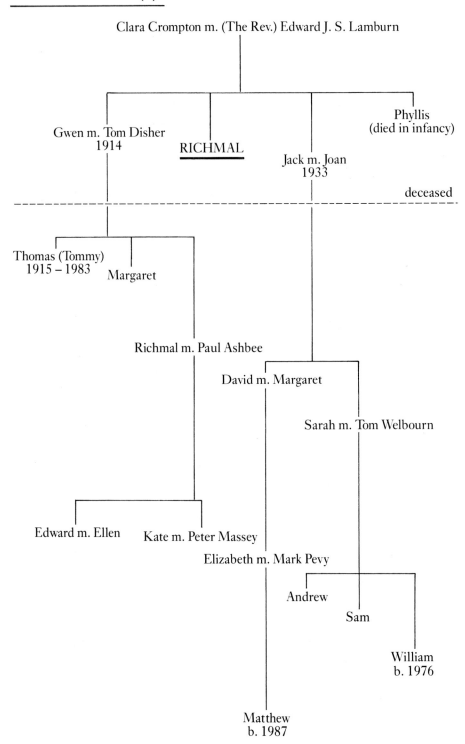

Clara Crompton m. (The Rev.) Edward J. S. Lamburn

Gwen m. Tom Disher
1914

RICHMAL

Jack m. Joan
1933

Phyllis
(died in infancy)

deceased

Thomas (Tommy)
1915 – 1983

Margaret

Richmal m. Paul Ashbee

David m. Margaret

Sarah m. Tom Welbourn

Edward m. Ellen

Kate m. Peter Massey

Elizabeth m. Mark Pevy

Andrew

Sam

William
b. 1976

Matthew
b. 1987

XIV

The Perfect Aunt

Aunt Richmal never met the only real-life William in our family: her great-nephew William Welbourn. Born in 1976 – seven years after Richmal's death – he is the youngest son of Jack Lamburn's daughter, Sarah.

There was a difference of 30 years between the oldest and the youngest of Richmal's nieces and nephews. Tommy and I were the eldest, followed by our much younger sister, Richmal Junior. After another four years came David, the first child of Jack's rather late marriage, who preceded his sister Sarah by ten years.

Our aunt adjusted easily from one age group to the other. Sarah gratefully recalls the sympathy and help she received when both her parents were ill in hospital at the same time and she was distraught with worry. In between hospital visits she had long phone conversations with Aunt Richmal ranging over many different subjects including reincarnation. Although Christians are supposed to believe in the Life Hereafter, most of our family believed that we had to come back again many times over.

We had an uncomfortable feeling that the Zen Buddhists were right. Not only were we working out the karmas of our previous lives in the journey to perfection but in this life we were building up a lot of trouble for the next time round. I told Auntie very firmly that in my next life I intend to be totally incompetent, a completely helpless female, admiring everything done by other people until they offer to take over my share of the work. I shall say, "How clever you are. How talented! You are so lucky, being able to do these things for yourself." Given sufficient praise and flattery, other people will wait on me hand and foot. Having managed in this life to follow the helpless policy for cooking, gardening and cars, I shall extend the idea for further development on my return visit. Auntie suspected that men had practised the technique for centuries and said I was sure to get my turn soon.

My mother and Richmal were deeply interested in religion; they used to buy books on the various philosophies and exchange them with each other. I found many shelves packed

William Welbourn, Richmal Crompton's great-nephew: 1990

with the books when I cleared our house; some hardback, some paperback, bought by all three after Tommy began to share their interest during the 1960s. There were books on Buddhism, the Rosicrucians, Christian Science and well known publications such as *The Imitation of Christ*, an early 18th-century edition of the English translation. The two sisters used to discuss matters of belief, including the Muslim and Hebrew faiths, over pots of tea or glasses of sherry, puffing away at their tipped Craven A's.

As a family we believed there might be some form of thought transference between people on the same wavelength. We tried experiments of concentrated thought to make other members of the family – or friends – pick up the phone and ring us. Sometimes it was successful, sometimes not. Several times Richmal produced a novel that had much the same basic plot as another well known woman writer's, published at around the same time. Richmal's publisher suggested she should write at a different time of the year to inspire a different plot; but this was not easy for someone like Richmal who wrote all through the year and whose plots were not necessarily formulated at the start. The only answer was for the two authors to get in touch and compare ideas, which they did to mutual enlightenment; but they could not decide whether their plot similarities had been thought transference or mere coincidence.

Richmal had a good agent but even he could not undo a serious error she made in the early years when handling her own work; she sold the copyright of the first two William books – *Just-William* and *More William* – outright to Newnes. The agent managed to negotiate an ex-gratia payment but it was a drop in the ocean compared with the royalties she would have earned on these two books, which were re-issued many times during her lifetime.

I suspect that a lot of people borrowed money from Aunt Richmal. She was a sitting target for begging letters, also appeals from friends – and relatives. There were, of course, lots of sycophants aound her. Being an extremely generous person she must have given away much of her earnings, not only to charities. Yet she was quite mean with herself, never extravagant. Through the influence of her father's teaching she felt it was wicked to spend much money on her own food, clothes and worldly goods. "Showing off" was no part of her life, her only extravagances being for other people. Throughout her life she followed the family tradition of giving a percentage of her earnings to charity.

Travel was a different matter; she considered it a challenge in overcoming her disability. She had an intense curiosity about other people, other nationalities and races. Eager to see all the places she had read about, she explored as much of Europe as possible, mainly Italy and France, and was disappointed not to reach more of the lands of her classical studies. She was usually accompanied by one or two friends, since there was always the risk that she might damage her "good" leg and therefore need help. And after spending hours walking around historical ruins, churches and museums she was no doubt glad of a friendly arm. However, it was possible to take short cruises on her own – a comparatively safe mode of travel, with a ship's crew to help if necessary. She went to Iceland and was fascinated by the hot springs and geysers against a backdrop of rather bleak volcanic scenery, a stark comparison with Europe. On one occasion she attended the Oberammagau Passion Play and in the 1960s became friendly with an East German woman who took her travelling into West Germany; only now do I wonder how that friend came to be allowed out of the Eastern zone so often, and to visit Britain from time to time. It may have been because she was a teacher. Or were her supervisory Comrades amongst the many fans of Just William? He certainly held some Communistic views.

Auntie always wanted to hear every detail of my own travels. She was intrigued by places like Istanbul and certainly interested in the USA and Canada. She would have enjoyed hearing about my adventures in the Middle East and countries behind the Iron Curtain, including Russia, but those travels took place several years after her death. When I raved about the beauty of the Austrian and Swiss mountains and in particular Bad Gastein's dramatic waterfall, which cascades through the centre of the town (one of the Hapsburgs' favourite spas), she wanted me to take her there. But sadly I realised she would not be able to walk in that town. Every step, even from shop to shop or from one hotel to another, was steeply up or steeply down and she would be certain to fall, however careful we were. In her time she experienced some serious falls but always made light of them. In my mind's eye I can still see her face as she overbalanced backwards from the raised path to our house. I was standing right beside her and caught a fleeting glimpse of her expression which conveyed an appeal: "Help me!" Quickly I stretched out my arm but it was too late. I failed to stop that fall and the memory still haunts me.

Richmal would often make an absurd statement with a totally serious face. In fact our conversations were rarely serious, except when fate dealt me unfortunate cards and she tried to console me. She used to say that events which appear to be dreadful calamities at the time often prove to be a turning point towards something better, and that looking back later one thinks, "If that hadn't happened – and it seemed so awful at the time – then I would never have gone along the present route, which has turned out so much better." This philosophy had certainly proved true for her; she always claimed to have had a much more interesting life as a writer – the result of her catching polio – than she could have had as a schoolteacher.

It was my mother who used to say: "When one door closes another usually opens but you have to be out in the corridor to see it." I have found this to be true, although for me several doors usually open at the same time and generally I try to charge through the lot at once. Aunt Richmal was heard to say "Margaret is like a rubber ball. She goes right down and then immediately bounces up again." In following years I was often grateful for that comment; every time I went down I remembered to be a rubber ball and struggled to come up again quickly.

After I had decided to close down two business ventures in the early 1960s, a whole new vista opened up almost immediately. Most of my working life I had run a double career, quite separately – as a designer and as a technical journalist. Now, in addition to writing for a new journal just starting up, I took on the design of uniforms for a small airline, then the state midwives and – to my joy, because I had always loved trains – British Rail. But as usual I ended up with too much work, and had to take some with me every time I went home. Fortunately Aunt Richmal was an exact size 12, so I pressed her into service.

"What am I today?" she would ask as I made her undress. One time I said "You are a waitress in the formal restaurant at the new Euston station, which the Queen is opening in two months' time." On another occasion: "You are a British Rail nurse – I bet you didn't know British Rail employed their own nurses!" She loved these transformation scenes. Sometimes she was a Hovercraft purserette or a hotel housekeeper, even a ship's stewardess. When I turned her into a British Transport policewoman she tried to look officious, making sure there was enough space in her jacket pockets for notebook, radio and whistle. "There is no room for my hankie," she complained. The whole family then joined in, suggesting polite (and other) places where she could keep her hankie. Best of all she liked the idea of moulded outfits cooked in a huge oven, an advanced manufacturing technique I developed during the few months before she died. She was looking forward to saying "I'll just go and get my dress out of the oven." But she never saw the final result, launched later in 1969. Had she lived into the 1970s she could have been an East African Airways stewardess, a Libyan Arab Airways hostess and – best of all – a Gulf Air cabin-crew member. However, she was around long enough to inspect my writings on machinery and hear the first siren calls of the computers.

Our two schoolmistress supervisors, Mother and Richmal, had been more successful in correcting my use of grammar than Tommy's. His pronunciation of words was also quite inventive. Naturally we both made many mistakes and I still remember my youthful humiliation as a child when reading aloud to Auntie a paragraph describing a man's moustache; I pronounced it like toothache, and she laughed until she nearly cried. All my life I have pitied foreign students trying to learn English, and was always thankful that I had two mentors whom I could phone for instant help. One or other could usually answer any questions I threw at them, which was quicker than locating an encyclopaedia. It was often a matter of obscure history, such as "What exactly did Jezebel do?" Except for Latin at school and a smattering of French Tommy had failed to master any foreign language; it took all his time and effort to learn our own. What did it matter anyway, as long as we understood each other? When abroad in the army he had learned some very effective sign language, most of which he refused to show us.

I often turned to Richmal for help in writing. One time I wanted to know the correct use of the colon in comparison with the semicolon; on that occasion she looked up various authorities on punctuation and wrote me a long letter which, however, failed to cure my devotion to semicolons. She took a great interest in my education even in adult years. After I had seen the "Lawrence of Arabia" film she gave me a selection of books I should read. This other Thomas Edward, a non-conformist like our own Thomas Edward, had been more successful in finding his mission in life despite going adrift at times. Richmal wrote: "I enclose The Letters (*Selected Letters of T.E. Lawrence*). I think, like me, you'll be a bit bored by the Archaeology section. I found The Years of Hide and Seek, also Speed Boats, more interesting – but they may possibly be a bit too lit'ry for you. He *was* actually a lit'ry gent as well as a soldier and you get all the soldiering in The Pillars. I've just rung up the Army & Navy Stores to ask about the other book I ordered. They seem vague and are going to ring me back later. It may be out of print but if so I will get another on the list." Sometimes she addressed me as Dearest M, sometimes as Darling M, but I was always M. Her handwriting was generally irregular and disjointed, possibly influenced by Greek lettering, and the letters I received

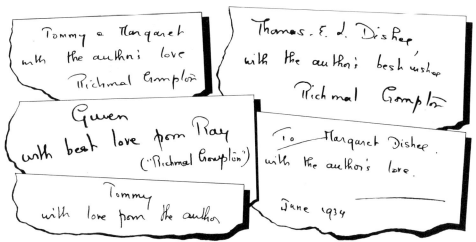

Richmal always gave first editions, duly autographed, to members of the family

Her writing became more difficult to read as the years passed

during the few years before her death – always written hurriedly – were rather difficult to read.

Richmal and I shared a number of interests, including Chinese Art and Egyptology, and we were excited in 1937 to visit a special Chinese Art exhibition in London. After Clara's death, when I was working in London, we used to meet for lunch fairly frequently, generally at one of Auntie's clubs – either one in Cavendish Square or another in Berkeley Street. I had little time but could just manage lunch as long as we were served quickly. During one of these meetings, in 1939, I was more than surprised when she suggested I should share Ding's flat just off Charing Cross Road. Ding was the scenery designer, real name Leon Davey, a good friend of Richmal's and only in his thirties.

Eventually I moved in. Ding was on night duty in Civil Defence and as I was working during the day we managed to share his flat without catching sight of each other. He used to leave me notes: "Dear Lodger, You don't seem to be eating anything for breakfast. There are some plums in a bowl in the cupboard. Help yourself." I replied: "Dear Landlord, Many thanks for your offer but I have breakfast in a café near where I work. Really, I'm not starving." Then the crisis came: "Dear Landlord. I'm terribly sorry but I've pulled the bathroom rail out of the wall. I can't get it back again." "Dear Lodger. That's quite all right. It's always happening. I've fixed it." Ding was called up for the Navy after two or three months of this domestic bliss, so had to give up the flat and finally we met again when he was packing up and I moved out. We were not even ships that passed in the night.

Richmal had come much more frequently to our Bromley house after Clara's death, often staying for the evening meal to be there when Tommy and I came back from work. Then when the war started we packed up and moved into The Glebe, making it our base for several years. Following in our footsteps, Jack and his family took our place living with Richmal, so she was not really alone until 1945. Her faithful daily Mrs Watts looked after her but the house was really too large for one person. Although Auntie liked gardening and had the help of a local character named Westbrook for at least one day a week, the large garden was also proving too much.

Richmal had been surprised to find that she enjoyed being alone, free to think her own thoughts without interruption.

At the photographer's request Richmal posed at this desk
but she normally worked at a table in her study

She was by temperament a loner – like her brother Jack, who stayed most of the day and well into the night alone in the attic of his house, writing books and reading, while his family ran their lives in the rest of the house. But the loners still enjoyed parties, providing they could be sure some kindred spirits would be around. And, of course, Richmal had a subconscious need to study people and their funny ways.

So the time came for Richmal to part with The Glebe, much to our sorrow. She wanted a smaller house without stairs, which she was finding more and more difficult to manage. She discovered a bungalow in Chislehurst which, although it held no charm for me, was considered suitable; it was still within easy reach of Bromley and on the direct railway route to London. She moved house in 1954, having sold The Glebe for about five thousand pounds to a scrap-metal merchant.

**Animated party repartee. Richmal manages to hold stick,
fur jacket, large handbag, gloves and wine glass**

The next purchaser for The Glebe, quite a few years later, was a German who had plans to demolish the house and build a small housing estate in its place. The present owner told me: "I was desperate to get the house from the German, to stop him pulling it down. My husband and I were thrilled when he agreed our price and we moved in. Unfortunately my husband died a few years later but I, my daughter and family are very happy living here." They have added two extra garages and combined several rooms to make extra space. The garden is now less formal – in my view an improvement – yet I miss some of our favourite trees at the front, our watchtowers. The place is guarded now with an illusion of twenty dogs barking the moment anyone approaches the house. I feel like saying, "Stop barking! This is William's house – and Auntie Ray's and Clara's – and all their visitors, the great-aunts, the cousins, the Dishers and the Lamburns. I am the only one left from when they built the house. Don't bark at me."

Although Clara had died at The Glebe, after several previous heart attacks, Richmal had experienced only one illness there. It was the Chislehurst bungalow, Beechworth, that witnessed her broken "good" leg and the two coronary thromboses. The first coronary, in 1960, was a shock to all of us. She had been regarded as delicate in her childhood, but as an adult was more resilient than she looked and had shown no signs of heart trouble. So her sudden removal to Farnborough Hospital had a very sobering effect on all of us. For a while she hovered on the brink, but fortunately recovered sufficiently to move back to the Chislehurst house on the understanding that she would have a full-time housekeeper-companion for at least six months. At first Richmal was not even allowed to lift her arms above her head to do her hair, so a suitably qualified and kind companion was found to help her during that time while she gradually returned to normal life. At the end of six months, the companion left for Australia to live with her brother and Richmal returned to the loner status she so much enjoyed, still looked after by Mrs Watts.

Thinking Auntie was still in need of help, I asked a friend of mine living within striking distance of Beechworth to call on her. I was secretly hoping that this friend would do some of the shopping. But unknown to me she was in the middle of a marriage crisis and arrived on the doorstep with tears streaming down her face and clutching a bottle of gin. The two of them had several gin-and-tears sessions, during which she poured out her sad and dramatic story and found consolation in Richmal's sympathy. I think she was Agony Aunt to quite a number of people over the years but this particular scene was not at all what I had envisaged.

We all thought of Richmal as a lovely kind aunt who was always amusing and invariably interested in whatever we were doing. Without exception she put others first and herself last. To this day I cannot assess to what extent she covered her true feelings by exercising strong self-control. I only witnessed one situation that really made her cry; but it was not on her own account. When alone she must have cried over the illnesses and deaths of friends and relatives. Yet she

The two sisters: Gwen and Richmal in the mid-1960s

was always the first to comfort the rest of us. On the rare occasions that she became angry, it was always in defence of someone else who had been unjustly treated. Once when I had shown anger, she asked me why I had behaved in that way. "Because I wanted to show that I was angry, so it would have been silly to cover it up." We then proceeded to a calm discussion on the reasons for showing or hiding anger and the situations in which one technique or the other might be appropriate.

She used to give marvellous presents to all of us – although it was particularly difficult to make the right choice for Tommy, to whom honesty was sacrosanct, whatever the embarrassment he might cause. On one of his birthdays she gave him a battery razor, which he studied carefully, but he could not imagine its place in his own life. He thanked her politely but added that he already possessed a razor. She explained that he could now shave in the office, which he countered with a firm rejection: he would not be allowed to do that. Then she suggested he might want to shave on the train, which idea appalled him. In any case, he shaved every morning before starting out. She became increasingly desperate. "The leaflet says you can shave on a desert island." He replied, "If I were on a desert island, I wouldn't shave. I'd grow a beard." In the end she had to take the razor back to the shop and find something else – inevitably, golf balls.

Richmal was writing the 39th William book when she had the second coronary and died soon afterwards in hospital, on January 11th 1969, at the age of 78. She had seemed reasonably well the day before but thought she might be sickening for 'flu. Early on Saturday the 11th she had phoned friends nearby for help. They called a doctor and she was taken by ambulance to Farnborough Hospital, where she died a few hours later. It was all so sudden that none of the family could reach her in time to be with her at the end.

William carries on and no one would have been more surprised at that than Richmal herself, who assumed that with her death he would fade from the scene. He was, of course, part of our family and to us very real. That can probably be said by other families amongst his fans, whose love of William has been handed down from grandparents via parents to today's children, in the many countries where the translated editions are available. On the other hand there are today a considerable number of young people who have never heard of William, which is very much their loss.

POSTSCRIPT

WHERE WAS WILLIAM'S VILLAGE?

Excerpt from letter by Mr. John Teed, published in *The Independent* April 12th 1990:

"As a boy I knew Miss Richmal Crompton Lamburn well. She lived quietly with her mother in Cherry Orchard Road, Bromley Common, three miles beyond Bromley, in Kent. My family lived next door. In those days, 70 years ago, it was a small rural village. Miss Lamburn was a delightful unassuming young woman and I used to play with her young nephew, Tommy. He used to get up to all sorts of tricks, and he was always presumed to be the inspiration for 'William' by us all.

"Miss Lamburn started writing short stories after she has been forced to give up teaching, having contracted polio . . . Owing to her restricted movements she took her setting from her immediate surroundings, which contained many of the features described, such as unspoilt woods and wide streams and Biggin Hill Aerodrome, very active in the Twenties . . . It was Bromley Common – I was there so I know."

John Teed
Bradford on Avon,
Wiltshire

Richmal as John Teed would have known her

Comment by Councillor R. L. Ainsby, Mayor of Bromley 1989-1990, in his foreword to *Undaunted*, Graham Reeves' story of Bromley in World War II:

"As an avid *Just-William* reader when young, and for many years having lived near Oakley Road, the home of Richmal Crompton, I have long believed that the stories were set in that area. The stream in the wood where the Outlaws played was the Ravensbourne in Barnet Wood and the 'Big' houses were The Cedars and Hollydale, alas now gone. The Church was Holy Trinity and the fields and farm were Oakley House."

Undaunted, published by Bromley Leisure Services, includes a William story written by Richmal Crompton for the Civil Defence magazine of December 1939 in which a rehearsal for the capture of spies of Bromley's Civil Defence is misunderstood by William, who takes it for a genuine spy ring.

Richmal in the 1950s

Margaret carries on walking.
The baby Tommy tried to lose,
now a bit older. 1990

THIS BOOK IS DEDICATED TO

Tommy – the companion of my youth
and
the happy memory of Auntie Ray
to celebrate the Centenary
Anniversary in 1990 of her birth

Richmal C. Lamburn